ISBN 0-8373-2931-0

C-2931 CAREER EXAMINATION SERIES

# *This is your PASSBOOK® for...*

# Senior Caseworker

## *Test Preparation Study Guide*

## *Questions & Answers*

NATIONAL LEARNING CORPORATION

Copyright © 2016 by

# National Learning Corporation

## 212 Michael Drive, Syosset, New York 11791

(516) 921-8888
(800) 645-6337
FAX: (516) 921-8743
www.passbooks.com
sales @ passbooks.com
info @ passbooks.com

PRINTED IN THE UNITED STATES OF AMERICA

# PASSBOOK®
## NOTICE

# PASSBOOK® SERIES

THE *PASSBOOK® SERIES* has been created to prepare applicants and candidates for the ultimate academic battlefield – the examination room.

At some time in our lives, each and every one of us may be required to take an examination – for validation, matriculation, admission, qualification, registration, certification, or licensure.

Based on the assumption that every applicant or candidate has met the basic formal educational standards, has taken the required number of courses, and read the necessary texts, the *PASSBOOK® SERIES* furnishes the one special preparation which may assure passing with confidence, instead of failing with insecurity. Examination questions – together with answers – are furnished as the basic vehicle for study so that the mysteries of the examination and its compounding difficulties may be eliminated or diminished by a sure method.

This book is meant to help you pass your examination provided that you qualify and are serious in your objective.

The entire field is reviewed through the huge store of content information which is succinctly presented through a provocative and challenging approach – the question-and-answer method.

A climate of success is established by furnishing the correct answers at the end of each test.

You soon learn to recognize types of questions, forms of questions, and patterns of questioning. You may even begin to anticipate expected outcomes.

You perceive that many questions are repeated or adapted so that you can gain acute insights, which may enable you to score many sure points.

You learn how to confront new questions, or types of questions, and to attack them confidently and work out the correct answers.

You note objectives and emphases, and recognize pitfalls and dangers, so that you may make positive educational adjustments.

Moreover, you are kept fully informed in relation to new concepts, methods, practices, and directions in the field.

You discover that you are actually taking the examination all the time: you are preparing for the examination by "taking" an examination, not by reading extraneous and/or supererogatory textbooks.

In short, this PASSBOOK®, used directedly, should be an important factor in helping you to pass your test.

# SENIOR CASEWORKER

DUTIES

Assists Casework Supervisors in management of a casework unit. Reviews routine correspondence initiated by Caseworkers for acceptability and conformance with agency policy. Assists in instruction of newly assigned Caseworkers in general policies, procedures and services of agency. Handles controversial, unusual, difficult and complex cases; dictates and maintains case records. Participates in conferences with departmental, public and private agencies to interpret departmental functions and services relating to specific referrals and planned details of cooperative services. Performs related work as required.

SCOPE OF THE EXAMINATION

The written test will be designed to test for knowledge, skills, and/or abilities in such areas as:

1. Principles and practices of social casework;
2. Preparing written material;
3. Interviewing; and
4. Case histories in social services casework programs.

# HOW TO TAKE A TEST

## I. YOU MUST PASS AN EXAMINATION

### A. *WHAT EVERY CANDIDATE SHOULD KNOW*

Examination applicants often ask us for help in preparing for the written test. What can I study in advance? What kinds of questions will be asked? How will the test be given? How will the papers be graded?

As an applicant for a civil service examination, you may be wondering about some of these things. Our purpose here is to suggest effective methods of advance study and to describe civil service examinations.

Your chances for success on this examination can be increased if you know how to prepare. Those "pre-examination jitters" can be reduced if you know what to expect. You can even experience an adventure in good citizenship if you know why civil service exams are given.

### B. *WHY ARE CIVIL SERVICE EXAMINATIONS GIVEN?*

Civil service examinations are important to you in two ways. As a citizen, you want public jobs filled by employees who know how to do their work. As a job seeker, you want a fair chance to compete for that job on an equal footing with other candidates. The best-known means of accomplishing this two-fold goal is the competitive examination.

Exams are widely publicized throughout the nation. They may be administered for jobs in federal, state, city, municipal, town or village governments or agencies.

Any citizen may apply, with some limitations, such as the age or residence of applicants. Your experience and education may be reviewed to see whether you meet the requirements for the particular examination. When these requirements exist, they are reasonable and applied consistently to all applicants. Thus, a competitive examination may cause you some uneasiness now, but it is your privilege and safeguard.

### C. *HOW ARE CIVIL SERVICE EXAMS DEVELOPED?*

Examinations are carefully written by trained technicians who are specialists in the field known as "psychological measurement," in consultation with recognized authorities in the field of work that the test will cover. These experts recommend the subject matter areas or skills to be tested; only those knowledges or skills important to your success on the job are included. The most reliable books and source materials available are used as references. Together, the experts and technicians judge the difficulty level of the questions.

Test technicians know how to phrase questions so that the problem is clearly stated. Their ethics do not permit "trick" or "catch" questions. Questions may have been tried out on sample groups, or subjected to statistical analysis, to determine their usefulness.

Written tests are often used in combination with performance tests, ratings of training and experience, and oral interviews. All of these measures combine to form the best-known means of finding the right person for the right job.

## II. HOW TO PASS THE WRITTEN TEST

### A. NATURE OF THE EXAMINATION

To prepare intelligently for civil service examinations, you should know how they differ from school examinations you have taken. In school you were assigned certain definite pages to read or subjects to cover. The examination questions were quite detailed and usually emphasized memory. Civil service exams, on the other hand, try to discover your present ability to perform the duties of a position, plus your potentiality to learn these duties. In other words, a civil service exam attempts to predict how successful you will be. Questions cover such a broad area that they cannot be as minute and detailed as school exam questions.

In the public service similar kinds of work, or positions, are grouped together in one "class." This process is known as *position-classification*. All the positions in a class are paid according to the salary range for that class. One class title covers all of these positions, and they are all tested by the same examination.

### B. FOUR BASIC STEPS

#### 1) Study the announcement

How, then, can you know what subjects to study? Our best answer is: "Learn as much as possible about the class of positions for which you've applied." The exam will test the knowledge, skills and abilities needed to do the work.

Your most valuable source of information about the position you want is the official exam announcement. This announcement lists the training and experience qualifications. Check these standards and apply only if you come reasonably close to meeting them.

The brief description of the position in the examination announcement offers some clues to the subjects which will be tested. Think about the job itself. Review the duties in your mind. Can you perform them, or are there some in which you are rusty? Fill in the blank spots in your preparation.

Many jurisdictions preview the written test in the exam announcement by including a section called "Knowledge and Abilities Required," "Scope of the Examination," or some similar heading. Here you will find out specifically what fields will be tested.

#### 2) Review your own background

Once you learn in general what the position is all about, and what you need to know to do the work, ask yourself which subjects you already know fairly well and which need improvement. You may wonder whether to concentrate on improving your strong areas or on building some background in your fields of weakness. When the announcement has specified "some knowledge" or "considerable knowledge," or has used adjectives like "beginning principles of…" or "advanced … methods," you can get a clue as to the number and difficulty of questions to be asked in any given field. More questions, and hence broader coverage, would be included for those subjects which are more important in the work. Now weigh your strengths and weaknesses against the job requirements and prepare accordingly.

#### 3) Determine the level of the position

Another way to tell how intensively you should prepare is to understand the level of the job for which you are applying. Is it the entering level? In other words, is this the position in which beginners in a field of work are hired? Or is it an intermediate or advanced level? Sometimes this is indicated by such words as "Junior" or "Senior" in the class title. Other jurisdictions use Roman numerals to designate the level – Clerk I, Clerk II, for example. The word "Supervisor" sometimes appears in the title. If the level is not indicated by the title, check the description of duties. Will you be working under very close supervision, or will you have responsibility for independent decisions in this work?

## 4) Choose appropriate study materials

Now that you know the subjects to be examined and the relative amount of each subject to be covered, you can choose suitable study materials. For beginning level jobs, or even advanced ones, if you have a pronounced weakness in some aspect of your training, read a modern, standard textbook in that field. Be sure it is up to date and has general coverage. Such books are normally available at your library, and the librarian will be glad to help you locate one. For entry-level positions, questions of appropriate difficulty are chosen – neither highly advanced questions, nor those too simple. Such questions require careful thought but not advanced training.

If the position for which you are applying is technical or advanced, you will read more advanced, specialized material. If you are already familiar with the basic principles of your field, elementary textbooks would waste your time. Concentrate on advanced textbooks and technical periodicals. Think through the concepts and review difficult problems in your field.

These are all general sources. You can get more ideas on your own initiative, following these leads. For example, training manuals and publications of the government agency which employs workers in your field can be useful, particularly for technical and professional positions. A letter or visit to the government department involved may result in more specific study suggestions, and certainly will provide you with a more definite idea of the exact nature of the position you are seeking.


## III. KINDS OF TESTS

Tests are used for purposes other than measuring knowledge and ability to perform specified duties. For some positions, it is equally important to test ability to make adjustments to new situations or to profit from training. In others, basic mental abilities not dependent on information are essential. Questions which test these things may not appear as pertinent to the duties of the position as those which test for knowledge and information. Yet they are often highly important parts of a fair examination. For very general questions, it is almost impossible to help you direct your study efforts. What we can do is to point out some of the more common of these general abilities needed in public service positions and describe some typical questions.

### 1) General information

Broad, general information has been found useful for predicting job success in some kinds of work. This is tested in a variety of ways, from vocabulary lists to questions about current events. Basic background in some field of work, such as sociology or economics, may be sampled in a group of questions. Often these are principles which have become familiar to most persons through exposure rather than through formal training. It is difficult to advise you how to study for these questions; being alert to the world around you is our best suggestion.

### 2) Verbal ability

An example of an ability needed in many positions is verbal or language ability. Verbal ability is, in brief, the ability to use and understand words. Vocabulary and grammar tests are typical measures of this ability. Reading comprehension or paragraph interpretation questions are common in many kinds of civil service tests. You are given a paragraph of written material and asked to find its central meaning.

### 3) Numerical ability

Number skills can be tested by the familiar arithmetic problem, by checking paired lists of numbers to see which are alike and which are different, or by interpreting charts and graphs. In the latter test, a graph may be printed in the test booklet which you are asked to use as the basis for answering questions.

### 4) Observation

A popular test for law-enforcement positions is the observation test. A picture is shown to you for several minutes, then taken away. Questions about the picture test your ability to observe both details and larger elements.

### 5) Following directions

In many positions in the public service, the employee must be able to carry out written instructions dependably and accurately. You may be given a chart with several columns, each column listing a variety of information. The questions require you to carry out directions involving the information given in the chart.

### 6) Skills and aptitudes

Performance tests effectively measure some manual skills and aptitudes. When the skill is one in which you are trained, such as typing or shorthand, you can practice. These tests are often very much like those given in business school or high school courses. For many of the other skills and aptitudes, however, no short-time preparation can be made. Skills and abilities natural to you or that you have developed throughout your lifetime are being tested.

Many of the general questions just described provide all the data needed to answer the questions and ask you to use your reasoning ability to find the answers. Your best preparation for these tests, as well as for tests of facts and ideas, is to be at your physical and mental best. You, no doubt, have your own methods of getting into an exam-taking mood and keeping "in shape." The next section lists some ideas on this subject.

## IV. KINDS OF QUESTIONS

Only rarely is the "essay" question, which you answer in narrative form, used in civil service tests. Civil service tests are usually of the short-answer type. Full instructions for answering these questions will be given to you at the examination. But in case this is your first experience with short-answer questions and separate answer sheets, here is what you need to know:

### 1) Multiple-choice Questions

Most popular of the short-answer questions is the "multiple choice" or "best answer" question. It can be used, for example, to test for factual knowledge, ability to solve problems or judgment in meeting situations found at work.

A multiple-choice question is normally one of three types—

- It can begin with an incomplete statement followed by several possible endings. You are to find the one ending which *best* completes the statement, although some of the others may not be entirely wrong.
- It can also be a complete statement in the form of a question which is answered by choosing one of the statements listed.

- It can be in the form of a problem – again you select the best answer.

Here is an example of a multiple-choice question with a discussion which should give you some clues as to the method for choosing the right answer:

When an employee has a complaint about his assignment, the action which will *best* help him overcome his difficulty is to
   A.  discuss his difficulty with his coworkers
   B.  take the problem to the head of the organization
   C.  take the problem to the person who gave him the assignment
   D.  say nothing to anyone about his complaint

In answering this question, you should study each of the choices to find which is best. Consider choice "A" – Certainly an employee may discuss his complaint with fellow employees, but no change or improvement can result, and the complaint remains unresolved. Choice "B" is a poor choice since the head of the organization probably does not know what assignment you have been given, and taking your problem to him is known as "going over the head" of the supervisor. The supervisor, or person who made the assignment, is the person who can clarify it or correct any injustice. Choice "C" is, therefore, correct. To say nothing, as in choice "D," is unwise. Supervisors have and interest in knowing the problems employees are facing, and the employee is seeking a solution to his problem.

## 2) True/False Questions

The "true/false" or "right/wrong" form of question is sometimes used. Here a complete statement is given. Your job is to decide whether the statement is right or wrong.

SAMPLE: A roaming cell-phone call to a nearby city costs less than a non-roaming call to a distant city.

This statement is wrong, or false, since roaming calls are more expensive.
This is not a complete list of all possible question forms, although most of the others are variations of these common types. You will always get complete directions for answering questions. Be sure you understand *how* to mark your answers – ask questions until you do.

## V. RECORDING YOUR ANSWERS

Computer terminals are used more and more today for many different kinds of exams.
For an examination with very few applicants, you may be told to record your answers in the test booklet itself. Separate answer sheets are much more common. If this separate answer sheet is to be scored by machine – and this is often the case – it is highly important that you mark your answers correctly in order to get credit.
An electronic scoring machine is often used in civil service offices because of the speed with which papers can be scored. Machine-scored answer sheets must be marked with a pencil, which will be given to you. This pencil has a high graphite content which responds to the electronic scoring machine. As a matter of fact, stray dots may register as answers, so do not let your pencil rest on the answer sheet while you are pondering the correct answer. Also, if your pencil lead breaks or is otherwise defective, ask for another.

Since the answer sheet will be dropped in a slot in the scoring machine, be careful not to bend the corners or get the paper crumpled.

The answer sheet normally has five vertical columns of numbers, with 30 numbers to a column. These numbers correspond to the question numbers in your test booklet. After each number, going across the page are four or five pairs of dotted lines. These short dotted lines have small letters or numbers above them. The first two pairs may also have a "T" or "F" above the letters. This indicates that the first two pairs only are to be used if the questions are of the true-false type. If the questions are multiple choice, disregard the "T" and "F" and pay attention only to the small letters or numbers.

Answer your questions in the manner of the sample that follows:

32. The largest city in the United States is
    A. Washington, D.C.
    B. New York City
    C. Chicago
    D. Detroit
    E. San Francisco

1) Choose the answer you think is best. (New York City is the largest, so "B" is correct.)
2) Find the row of dotted lines numbered the same as the question you are answering. (Find row number 32)
3) Find the pair of dotted lines corresponding to the answer. (Find the pair of lines under the mark "B.")
4) Make a solid black mark between the dotted lines.

## VI. BEFORE THE TEST

Common sense will help you find procedures to follow to get ready for an examination. Too many of us, however, overlook these sensible measures. Indeed, nervousness and fatigue have been found to be the most serious reasons why applicants fail to do their best on civil service tests. Here is a list of reminders:

- Begin your preparation early – Don't wait until the last minute to go scurrying around for books and materials or to find out what the position is all about.
- Prepare continuously – An hour a night for a week is better than an all-night cram session. This has been definitely established. What is more, a night a week for a month will return better dividends than crowding your study into a shorter period of time.
- Locate the place of the exam – You have been sent a notice telling you when and where to report for the examination. If the location is in a different town or otherwise unfamiliar to you, it would be well to inquire the best route and learn something about the building.
- Relax the night before the test – Allow your mind to rest. Do not study at all that night. Plan some mild recreation or diversion; then go to bed early and get a good night's sleep.
- Get up early enough to make a leisurely trip to the place for the test – This way unforeseen events, traffic snarls, unfamiliar buildings, etc. will not upset you.
- Dress comfortably – A written test is not a fashion show. You will be known by number and not by name, so wear something comfortable.

- Leave excess paraphernalia at home – Shopping bags and odd bundles will get in your way. You need bring only the items mentioned in the official notice you received; usually everything you need is provided. Do not bring reference books to the exam. They will only confuse those last minutes and be taken away from you when in the test room.
- Arrive somewhat ahead of time – If because of transportation schedules you must get there very early, bring a newspaper or magazine to take your mind off yourself while waiting.
- Locate the examination room – When you have found the proper room, you will be directed to the seat or part of the room where you will sit. Sometimes you are given a sheet of instructions to read while you are waiting. Do not fill out any forms until you are told to do so; just read them and be prepared.
- Relax and prepare to listen to the instructions
- If you have any physical problem that may keep you from doing your best, be sure to tell the test administrator. If you are sick or in poor health, you really cannot do your best on the exam. You can come back and take the test some other time.

## VII. AT THE TEST

The day of the test is here and you have the test booklet in your hand. The temptation to get going is very strong. Caution! There is more to success than knowing the right answers. You must know how to identify your papers and understand variations in the type of short-answer question used in this particular examination. Follow these suggestions for maximum results from your efforts:

### 1) Cooperate with the monitor

The test administrator has a duty to create a situation in which you can be as much at ease as possible. He will give instructions, tell you when to begin, check to see that you are marking your answer sheet correctly, and so on. He is not there to guard you, although he will see that your competitors do not take unfair advantage. He wants to help you do your best.

### 2) Listen to all instructions

Don't jump the gun! Wait until you understand all directions. In most civil service tests you get more time than you need to answer the questions. So don't be in a hurry. Read each word of instructions until you clearly understand the meaning. Study the examples, listen to all announcements and follow directions. Ask questions if you do not understand what to do.

### 3) Identify your papers

Civil service exams are usually identified by number only. You will be assigned a number; you must not put your name on your test papers. Be sure to copy your number correctly. Since more than one exam may be given, copy your exact examination title.

### 4) Plan your time

Unless you are told that a test is a "speed" or "rate of work" test, speed itself is usually not important. Time enough to answer all the questions will be provided, but this does not mean that you have all day. An overall time limit has been set. Divide the total time (in minutes) by the number of questions to determine the approximate time you have for each question.

## 5) Do not linger over difficult questions

If you come across a difficult question, mark it with a paper clip (useful to have along) and come back to it when you have been through the booklet. One caution if you do this – be sure to skip a number on your answer sheet as well. Check often to be sure that you have not lost your place and that you are marking in the row numbered the same as the question you are answering.

## 6) Read the questions

Be sure you know what the question asks! Many capable people are unsuccessful because they failed to *read* the questions correctly.

## 7) Answer all questions

Unless you have been instructed that a penalty will be deducted for incorrect answers, it is better to guess than to omit a question.

## 8) Speed tests

It is often better NOT to guess on speed tests. It has been found that on timed tests people are tempted to spend the last few seconds before time is called in marking answers at random – without even reading them – in the hope of picking up a few extra points. To discourage this practice, the instructions may warn you that your score will be "corrected" for guessing. That is, a penalty will be applied. The incorrect answers will be deducted from the correct ones, or some other penalty formula will be used.

## 9) Review your answers

If you finish before time is called, go back to the questions you guessed or omitted to give them further thought. Review other answers if you have time.

## 10) Return your test materials

If you are ready to leave before others have finished or time is called, take ALL your materials to the monitor and leave quietly. Never take any test material with you. The monitor can discover whose papers are not complete, and taking a test booklet may be grounds for disqualification.


## VIII. EXAMINATION TECHNIQUES

1) Read the general instructions carefully. These are usually printed on the first page of the exam booklet. As a rule, these instructions refer to the timing of the examination; the fact that you should not start work until the signal and must stop work at a signal, etc. If there are any *special* instructions, such as a choice of questions to be answered, make sure that you note this instruction carefully.

2) When you are ready to start work on the examination, that is as soon as the signal has been given, read the instructions to each question booklet, underline any key words or phrases, such as *least, best, outline, describe* and the like. In this way you will tend to answer as requested rather than discover on reviewing your paper that you *listed without describing*, that you selected the *worst* choice rather than the *best* choice, etc.

3) If the examination is of the objective or multiple-choice type – that is, each question will also give a series of possible answers: A, B, C or D, and you are called upon to select the best answer and write the letter next to that answer on your answer paper – it is advisable to start answering each question in turn. There may be anywhere from 50 to 100 such questions in the three or four hours allotted and you can see how much time would be taken if you read through all the questions before beginning to answer any. Furthermore, if you come across a question or group of questions which you know would be difficult to answer, it would undoubtedly affect your handling of all the other questions.

4) If the examination is of the essay type and contains but a few questions, it is a moot point as to whether you should read all the questions before starting to answer any one. Of course, if you are given a choice – say five out of seven and the like – then it is essential to read all the questions so you can eliminate the two that are most difficult. If, however, you are asked to answer all the questions, there may be danger in trying to answer the easiest one first because you may find that you will spend too much time on it. The best technique is to answer the first question, then proceed to the second, etc.

5) Time your answers. Before the exam begins, write down the time it started, then add the time allowed for the examination and write down the time it must be completed, then divide the time available somewhat as follows:
   - If 3-1/2 hours are allowed, that would be 210 minutes. If you have 80 objective-type questions, that would be an average of 2-1/2 minutes per question. Allow yourself no more than 2 minutes per question, or a total of 160 minutes, which will permit about 50 minutes to review.
   - If for the time allotment of 210 minutes there are 7 essay questions to answer, that would average about 30 minutes a question. Give yourself only 25 minutes per question so that you have about 35 minutes to review.

6) The most important instruction is to *read each question* and make sure you know what is wanted. The second most important instruction is to *time yourself properly* so that you answer every question. The third most important instruction is to *answer every question*. Guess if you have to but include something for each question. Remember that you will receive no credit for a blank and will probably receive some credit if you write something in answer to an essay question. If you guess a letter – say "B" for a multiple-choice question – you may have guessed right. If you leave a blank as an answer to a multiple-choice question, the examiners may respect your feelings but it will not add a point to your score. Some exams may penalize you for wrong answers, so in such cases *only*, you may not want to guess unless you have some basis for your answer.

7) Suggestions
   a. Objective-type questions
      1. Examine the question booklet for proper sequence of pages and questions
      2. Read all instructions carefully
      3. Skip any question which seems too difficult; return to it after all other questions have been answered
      4. Apportion your time properly; do not spend too much time on any single question or group of questions

5. Note and underline key words – *all, most, fewest, least, best, worst, same, opposite,* etc.
6. Pay particular attention to negatives
7. Note unusual option, e.g., unduly long, short, complex, different or similar in content to the body of the question
8. Observe the use of "hedging" words – *probably, may, most likely,* etc.
9. Make sure that your answer is put next to the same number as the question
10. Do not second-guess unless you have good reason to believe the second answer is definitely more correct
11. Cross out original answer if you decide another answer is more accurate; do not erase until you are ready to hand your paper in
12. Answer all questions; guess unless instructed otherwise
13. Leave time for review

b. Essay questions
1. Read each question carefully
2. Determine exactly what is wanted. Underline key words or phrases.
3. Decide on outline or paragraph answer
4. Include many different points and elements unless asked to develop any one or two points or elements
5. Show impartiality by giving pros and cons unless directed to select one side only
6. Make and write down any assumptions you find necessary to answer the questions
7. Watch your English, grammar, punctuation and choice of words
8. Time your answers; don't crowd material

8) Answering the essay question

Most essay questions can be answered by framing the specific response around several key words or ideas. Here are a few such key words or ideas:

M's: manpower, materials, methods, money, management
P's: purpose, program, policy, plan, procedure, practice, problems, pitfalls, personnel, public relations

a. Six basic steps in handling problems:
1. Preliminary plan and background development
2. Collect information, data and facts
3. Analyze and interpret information, data and facts
4. Analyze and develop solutions as well as make recommendations
5. Prepare report and sell recommendations
6. Install recommendations and follow up effectiveness

b. Pitfalls to avoid
1. *Taking things for granted* – A statement of the situation does not necessarily imply that each of the elements is necessarily true; for example, a complaint may be invalid and biased so that all that can be taken for granted is that a complaint has been registered

2. *Considering only one side of a situation* – Wherever possible, indicate several alternatives and then point out the reasons you selected the best one
3. *Failing to indicate follow up* – Whenever your answer indicates action on your part, make certain that you will take proper follow-up action to see how successful your recommendations, procedures or actions turn out to be
4. *Taking too long in answering any single question* – Remember to time your answers properly


## IX. AFTER THE TEST

Scoring procedures differ in detail among civil service jurisdictions although the general principles are the same. Whether the papers are hand-scored or graded by machine we have described, they are nearly always graded by number. That is, the person who marks the paper knows only the number – never the name – of the applicant. Not until all the papers have been graded will they be matched with names. If other tests, such as training and experience or oral interview ratings have been given, scores will be combined. Different parts of the examination usually have different weights. For example, the written test might count 60 percent of the final grade, and a rating of training and experience 40 percent. In many jurisdictions, veterans will have a certain number of points added to their grades.

After the final grade has been determined, the names are placed in grade order and an eligible list is established. There are various methods for resolving ties between those who get the same final grade – probably the most common is to place first the name of the person whose application was received first. Job offers are made from the eligible list in the order the names appear on it. You will be notified of your grade and your rank as soon as all these computations have been made. This will be done as rapidly as possible.

People who are found to meet the requirements in the announcement are called "eligibles." Their names are put on a list of eligible candidates. An eligible's chances of getting a job depend on how high he stands on this list and how fast agencies are filling jobs from the list.

When a job is to be filled from a list of eligibles, the agency asks for the names of people on the list of eligibles for that job. When the civil service commission receives this request, it sends to the agency the names of the three people highest on this list. Or, if the job to be filled has specialized requirements, the office sends the agency the names of the top three persons who meet these requirements from the general list.

The appointing officer makes a choice from among the three people whose names were sent to him. If the selected person accepts the appointment, the names of the others are put back on the list to be considered for future openings.

That is the rule in hiring from all kinds of eligible lists, whether they are for typist, carpenter, chemist, or something else. For every vacancy, the appointing officer has his choice of any one of the top three eligibles on the list. This explains why the person whose name is on top of the list sometimes does not get an appointment when some of the persons lower on the list do. If the appointing officer chooses the second or third eligible, the No. 1 eligible does not get a job at once, but stays on the list until he is appointed or the list is terminated.

## X. HOW TO PASS THE INTERVIEW TEST

The examination for which you applied requires an oral interview test. You have already taken the written test and you are now being called for the interview test – the final part of the formal examination.

You may think that it is not possible to prepare for an interview test and that there are no procedures to follow during an interview. Our purpose is to point out some things you can do in advance that will help you and some good rules to follow and pitfalls to avoid while you are being interviewed.

*What is an interview supposed to test?*

The written examination is designed to test the technical knowledge and competence of the candidate; the oral is designed to evaluate intangible qualities, not readily measured otherwise, and to establish a list showing the relative fitness of each candidate – as measured against his competitors – for the position sought. Scoring is not on the basis of "right" and "wrong," but on a sliding scale of values ranging from "not passable" to "outstanding." As a matter of fact, it is possible to achieve a relatively low score without a single "incorrect" answer because of evident weakness in the qualities being measured.

Occasionally, an examination may consist entirely of an oral test – either an individual or a group oral. In such cases, information is sought concerning the technical knowledges and abilities of the candidate, since there has been no written examination for this purpose. More commonly, however, an oral test is used to supplement a written examination.

*Who conducts interviews?*

The composition of oral boards varies among different jurisdictions. In nearly all, a representative of the personnel department serves as chairman. One of the members of the board may be a representative of the department in which the candidate would work. In some cases, "outside experts" are used, and, frequently, a businessman or some other representative of the general public is asked to serve. Labor and management or other special groups may be represented. The aim is to secure the services of experts in the appropriate field.

However the board is composed, it is a good idea (and not at all improper or unethical) to ascertain in advance of the interview who the members are and what groups they represent. When you are introduced to them, you will have some idea of their backgrounds and interests, and at least you will not stutter and stammer over their names.

*What should be done before the interview?*

While knowledge about the board members is useful and takes some of the surprise element out of the interview, there is other preparation which is more substantive. It *is* possible to prepare for an oral interview – in several ways:

## 1) Keep a copy of your application and review it carefully before the interview

This may be the only document before the oral board, and the starting point of the interview. Know what education and experience you have listed there, and the sequence and dates of all of it. Sometimes the board will ask you to review the highlights of your experience for them; you should not have to hem and haw doing it.

## 2) Study the class specification and the examination announcement

Usually, the oral board has one or both of these to guide them. The qualities, characteristics or knowledges required by the position sought are stated in these documents. They offer valuable clues as to the nature of the oral interview. For example, if the job involves supervisory responsibilities, the announcement will usually indicate that knowledge of modern supervisory methods and the qualifications of the candidate as a supervisor will be tested. If so, you can expect such questions, frequently in the form of a hypothetical situation which you are expected to solve. NEVER go into an oral without knowledge of the duties and responsibilities of the job you seek.

## 3) Think through each qualification required

Try to visualize the kind of questions you would ask if you were a board member. How well could you answer them? Try especially to appraise your own knowledge and background in each area, *measured against the job sought*, and identify any areas in which you are weak. Be critical and realistic – do not flatter yourself.

## 4) Do some general reading in areas in which you feel you may be weak

For example, if the job involves supervision and your past experience has NOT, some general reading in supervisory methods and practices, particularly in the field of human relations, might be useful. Do NOT study agency procedures or detailed manuals. The oral board will be testing your understanding and capacity, not your memory.

## 5) Get a good night's sleep and watch your general health and mental attitude

You will want a clear head at the interview. Take care of a cold or any other minor ailment, and of course, no hangovers.

*What should be done on the day of the interview?*

Now comes the day of the interview itself. Give yourself plenty of time to get there. Plan to arrive somewhat ahead of the scheduled time, particularly if your appointment is in the fore part of the day. If a previous candidate fails to appear, the board might be ready for you a bit early. By early afternoon an oral board is almost invariably behind schedule if there are many candidates, and you may have to wait. Take along a book or magazine to read, or your application to review, but leave any extraneous material in the waiting room when you go in for your interview. In any event, relax and compose yourself.

The matter of dress is important. The board is forming impressions about you – from your experience, your manners, your attitude, and your appearance. Give your personal appearance careful attention. Dress your best, but not your flashiest. Choose conservative, appropriate clothing, and be sure it is immaculate. This is a business interview, and your appearance should indicate that you regard it as such. Besides, being well groomed and properly dressed will help boost your confidence.

Sooner or later, someone will call your name and escort you into the interview room. *This is it.* From here on you are on your own. It is too late for any more preparation. But remember, you asked for this opportunity to prove your fitness, and you are here because your request was granted.

*What happens when you go in?*

The usual sequence of events will be as follows: The clerk (who is often the board stenographer) will introduce you to the chairman of the oral board, who will introduce you to the other members of the board. Acknowledge the introductions before you sit down. Do not be surprised if you find a microphone facing you or a stenotypist sitting by. Oral interviews are usually recorded in the event of an appeal or other review.

Usually the chairman of the board will open the interview by reviewing the highlights of your education and work experience from your application – primarily for the benefit of the other members of the board, as well as to get the material into the record. Do not interrupt or comment unless there is an error or significant misinterpretation; if that is the case, do not hesitate. But do not quibble about insignificant matters. Also, he will usually ask you some question about your education, experience or your present job – partly to get you to start talking and to establish the interviewing "rapport." He may start the actual questioning, or turn it over to one of the other members. Frequently, each member undertakes the questioning on a particular area, one in which he is perhaps most competent, so you can expect each member to participate in the examination. Because time is limited, you may also expect some rather abrupt switches in the direction the questioning takes, so do not be upset by it. Normally, a board member will not pursue a single line of questioning unless he discovers a particular strength or weakness.

After each member has participated, the chairman will usually ask whether any member has any further questions, then will ask you if you have anything you wish to add. Unless you are expecting this question, it may floor you. Worse, it may start you off on an extended, extemporaneous speech. The board is not usually seeking more information. The question is principally to offer you a last opportunity to present further qualifications or to indicate that you have nothing to add. So, if you feel that a significant qualification or characteristic has been overlooked, it is proper to point it out in a sentence or so. Do not compliment the board on the thoroughness of their examination – they have been sketchy, and you know it. If you wish, merely say, "No thank you, I have nothing further to add." This is a point where you can "talk yourself out" of a good impression or fail to present an important bit of information. Remember, *you close the interview yourself.*

The chairman will then say, "That is all, Mr. _____, thank you." Do not be startled; the interview is over, and quicker than you think. Thank him, gather your belongings and take your leave. Save your sigh of relief for the other side of the door.


*How to put your best foot forward*
Throughout this entire process, you may feel that the board individually and collectively is trying to pierce your defenses, seek out your hidden weaknesses and embarrass and confuse you. Actually, this is not true. They are obliged to make an appraisal of your qualifications for the job you are seeking, and they want to see you in your best light. Remember, they must interview all candidates and a non-cooperative candidate may become a failure in spite of their best efforts to bring out his qualifications. Here are 15 suggestions that will help you:

## 1) Be natural – Keep your attitude confident, not cocky
If you are not confident that you can do the job, do not expect the board to be. Do not apologize for your weaknesses, try to bring out your strong points. The board is interested in a positive, not negative, presentation. Cockiness will antagonize any board member and make him wonder if you are covering up a weakness by a false show of strength.

## 2) Get comfortable, but don't lounge or sprawl
Sit erectly but not stiffly. A careless posture may lead the board to conclude that you are careless in other things, or at least that you are not impressed by the importance of the occasion. Either conclusion is natural, even if incorrect. Do not fuss with your clothing, a pencil or an ashtray. Your hands may occasionally be useful to emphasize a point; do not let them become a point of distraction.

## 3) Do not wisecrack or make small talk
This is a serious situation, and your attitude should show that you consider it as such. Further, the time of the board is limited – they do not want to waste it, and neither should you.

## 4) Do not exaggerate your experience or abilities

In the first place, from information in the application or other interviews and sources, the board may know more about you than you think. Secondly, you probably will not get away with it. An experienced board is rather adept at spotting such a situation, so do not take the chance.

## 5) If you know a board member, do not make a point of it, yet do not hide it

Certainly you are not fooling him, and probably not the other members of the board. Do not try to take advantage of your acquaintanceship – it will probably do you little good.

## 6) Do not dominate the interview

Let the board do that. They will give you the clues – do not assume that you have to do all the talking. Realize that the board has a number of questions to ask you, and do not try to take up all the interview time by showing off your extensive knowledge of the answer to the first one.

## 7) Be attentive

You only have 20 minutes or so, and you should keep your attention at its sharpest throughout. When a member is addressing a problem or question to you, give him your undivided attention. Address your reply principally to him, but do not exclude the other board members.

## 8) Do not interrupt

A board member may be stating a problem for you to analyze. He will ask you a question when the time comes. Let him state the problem, and wait for the question.

## 9) Make sure you understand the question

Do not try to answer until you are sure what the question is. If it is not clear, restate it in your own words or ask the board member to clarify it for you. However, do not haggle about minor elements.

## 10) Reply promptly but not hastily

A common entry on oral board rating sheets is "candidate responded readily," or "candidate hesitated in replies." Respond as promptly and quickly as you can, but do not jump to a hasty, ill-considered answer.

## 11) Do not be peremptory in your answers

A brief answer is proper – but do not fire your answer back. That is a losing game from your point of view. The board member can probably ask questions much faster than you can answer them.

## 12) Do not try to create the answer you think the board member wants

He is interested in what kind of mind you have and how it works – not in playing games. Furthermore, he can usually spot this practice and will actually grade you down on it.

## 13) Do not switch sides in your reply merely to agree with a board member

Frequently, a member will take a contrary position merely to draw you out and to see if you are willing and able to defend your point of view. Do not start a debate, yet do not surrender a good position. If a position is worth taking, it is worth defending.

### 14) Do not be afraid to admit an error in judgment if you are shown to be wrong

The board knows that you are forced to reply without any opportunity for careful consideration. Your answer may be demonstrably wrong. If so, admit it and get on with the interview.

### 15) Do not dwell at length on your present job

The opening question may relate to your present assignment. Answer the question but do not go into an extended discussion. You are being examined for a *new* job, not your present one. As a matter of fact, try to phrase ALL your answers in terms of the job for which you are being examined.

*Basis of Rating*

Probably you will forget most of these "do's" and "don'ts" when you walk into the oral interview room. Even remembering them all will not ensure you a passing grade. Perhaps you did not have the qualifications in the first place. But remembering them will help you to put your best foot forward, without treading on the toes of the board members.

Rumor and popular opinion to the contrary notwithstanding, an oral board wants you to make the best appearance possible. They know you are under pressure – but they also want to see how you respond to it as a guide to what your reaction would be under the pressures of the job you seek. They will be influenced by the degree of poise you display, the personal traits you show and the manner in which you respond.

## ABOUT THIS BOOK

This book contains tests divided into Examination Sections. Go through each test, answering every question in the margin. We have also attached a sample answer sheet at the back of the book that can be removed and used. At the end of each test look at the answer key and check your answers. On the ones you got wrong, look at the right answer choice and learn. Do not fill in the answers first. Do not memorize the questions and answers, but understand the answer and principles involved. On your test, the questions will likely be different from the samples. Questions are changed and new ones added. If you understand these past questions you should have success with any changes that arise. Tests may consist of several types of questions. We have additional books on each subject should more study be advisable or necessary for you. Finally, the more you study, the better prepared you will be. This book is intended to be the last thing you study before you walk into the examination room. Prior study of relevant texts is also recommended. NLC publishes some of these in our Fundamental Series. Knowledge and good sense are important factors in passing your exam. Good luck also helps. So now study this Passbook, absorb the material contained within and take that knowledge into the examination. Then do your best to pass that exam.

———

# EXAMINATION SECTION

# EXAMINATION SECTION
# TEST 1

DIRECTIONS : Each question or incomplete statement is followed by several suggested answers or completions. Select the one that *BEST* answers the question or completes the statement. *PRINT THE LETTER OF THE CORRECT ANSWER IN THE SPACE AT THE RIGHT.*

1. When a worker is planning a future interview with a client, of the following, the *MOST* important consideration is the

    A. recommendations he will make to the client
    B. place where the client will be interviewed
    C. purpose for which the client will be interviewed
    D. personality of the client

1.\_\_\_\_

2. For a worker to make a practice of reviewing the client's case record, if available, prior to the interview, is usually

    A. *inadvisable,* because knowledge of the client's past record will tend to influence the worker's judgment
    B. *advisable,* because knowledge of the client's back-ground will help the worker to identify discrepancies in the client's responses
    C. *inadvisable,* because such review is time-consuming and of questionable value
    D. *advisable,* because knowledge of the client's back-ground will help the worker to understand the client's situation

2.\_\_\_\_

3. Assume that a worker makes a practice of constantly re-assuring clients with serious and complex problems by making such statements as: *I'm sure you'll soon be well; I know you'll get a job soon;* or *Everything will be all right.*
Of the following, the *most likely* result of such a practice is to

    A. encourage the client and make him feel that the worker understands what the client is going through
    B. make the client doubtful about the worker's understanding of his difficulties and the worker's ability to help
    C. confuse the client and cause him to hesitate to take any action on his own initiative
    D. help the client to be more realistic about his situation and the probability that it will improve

3.\_\_\_\_

4. In order to get the maximum amount of information from a client during an interview, of the following, it is *MOST* important for the worker to communicate to the client the feeling that the worker is

    A. interested in the client
    B. a figure of authority
    C. efficient in his work habits
    D. sympathetic to the client's life style

4.\_\_\_\_

5. Of the following, the worker who takes extremely detailed notes during an interview with     5.____
a client is *most likely* to

    A. encourage the client to talk freely
    B. distract and antagonize the client
    C. help the client feel at ease
    D. understand the client's feelings

6. You find that many of the clients you interview are verbally abusive and unusually hostile     6.____
to you.
Of the following, the *most appropriate* action for you to take *FIRST* is to

    A. review your interviewing techniques and consider whether you may be provoking
       these clients
    B. act in a more authoritative manner when interviewing troublesome clients
    C. tell these clients that you will not process their applications unless their trouble-
       some behavior ceases
    D. disregard the clients' troublesome behavior during the interviews

7. During an interview, you did not completely understand several of your client's     7.____
responses. In each instance, you rephrased the client's statement and asked the client if
that was what he meant.
For you to use such a technique during interviews would be considered

    A. *inappropriate;* you may have distorted the client's meaning by rephrasing his state-
       ments
    B. *inappropriate;* you should have asked the same question until you received a com-
       prehensible response
    C. *appropriate;* the client will have a chance to correct you if you have misinterpreted
       his responses
    D. *appropriate;* a worker should rephrase clients' responses for the records

8. A worker is interviewing a client who has just had a severe emotional shock because of     8.____
an assault on her by a mugger.
Of the following, the approach which would generally be *most helpful* to the client is for
the worker to

    A. comfort the client and encourage her to talk about the assault
    B. sympathize with the client but refuse to discuss the assault with her
    C. tell the client to control her emotions and think positively about the future
    D. proceed with the interview in an impersonal and un-emotional manner

9. A worker finds that her questions are misinterpreted by many of the clients she inter-     9.____
views.
Of the following, the *most likely* reason for this problem is that the

    A. client is not listening attentively
    B. client wants to avoid the subject being discussed
    C. worker has failed to express her meaning clearly
    D. worker has failed to put the client at ease

10. For a worker to look directly at the client and observe him during the interview is, gener-   10._____
ally,

    A. *inadvisable;* this will make the client nervous and uncomfortable
    B. *advisable;* the client will be more likely to refrain from lying
    C. *inadvisable;* the worker will not be able to take notes for the case record
    D. *advisable;* this will encourage conversation and accelerate the progress of the
       interview

11. You are interviewing a client who is applying for social services for the first time.   11._____
In order to encourage this client to freely give you the information needed for you to
establish his eligibility, of the following, the *BEST* way to *start* the interview is by

    A. asking questions the client can easily answer
    B. conveying the impression that his responses to your questions will be checked
    C. asking two or three similar but important questions
    D. assuring the client that your sole responsibility is *getting the facts*

12. Workers are encouraged to record significant information obtained from clients and ser-   12._____
vices provided for clients. Of the following, the *MOST* important reason for this practice is
that these case records will

    A. help to reduce the need for regular supervisory conferences
    B. indicate to workers which clients are taking up the most time
    C. provide information which will help the agency to improve its services to clients
    D. make it easier to verify the complaints of clients

13. As a worker in the employment eligibility section, you find that interviews can be com-   13._____
pleted in a shorter period of time if you ask questions which limit the client to a certain
answer.
For you to use such a technique would be considered

    A. *inappropriate,* because this type of question usually requires advance preparation
    B. *inappropriate,* because this type of question may inhibit the client from saying what
       he really means
    C. *appropriate,* because you know the areas into which the questions should be
       directed
    D. *appropriate,* because this type of question usually helps clients to express them-
       selves clearly

14. Assume that a worker at a juvenile detention center is planning foster care placement for    14.____
    a child.
    For the worker to have the child participate in the planning is generally considered to
    be

    A.   time-consuming and of little practical value in preparing the child for placement
    B.   valuable in helping the child adjust to future placement
    C.   useful, because the child will be more likely to cooperate with others in the center
    D.   anxiety-provoking, because the child will feel that he has been abandoned

15. You have been assigned to interview the mother of a five-year-old son in her home to get    15.____
    information useful in locating the child's absent father. During the interview, you notice
    many serious bruises on the child's arms and legs, which the mother explains are due to
    the child's clumsiness.
    Of the following, your BEST course of action is to

    A.   accept the mother's explanation and concentrate on getting information which will
         help you to locate the father
    B.   advise the mother to have the child examined for a medical condition that may be
         causing his clumsiness
    C.   make a surprise visit to the mother later, to see whether someone is beating the
         child
    D.   complete your interview with the mother and report the case to your supervisor for
         investigation of possible child abuse

16. During an interview, the former landlord of an absent father offers to help you to locate    16.____
    the father if you will give the landlord confidential information you have on the financial
    situation of the father.
    Of the following, you should

    A.   immediately end the interview with the landlord
    B.   urge the landlord to help you but explain that you are not permitted to give him con-
         fidential information
    C.   freely give the landlord the confidential information he requests about the father
    D.   give the landlord the information only if he promises to keep it confidential

17. You feel that your client, a released mental patient, is not adjusting well to living on his    17.____
    own in an apartment. To gather more information, you interview privately his next-door
    neighbor, who claims that the client is creating a *disturbance* and speaks of the client in
    an angry and insulting manner.
    Of the following, the BEST action for you to take in this situation is to

    A.   listen patiently to the neighbor to try to get the facts about your client's behavior
    B.   inform the neighbor that he has no right to speak insultingly about a mentally ill
         person
    C.   make an appointment to interview the neighbor some other time when he isn't so
         upset
    D.   tell the neighbor that you were not aware of the client's behavior and that you will
         have the client moved

18. As a worker assigned to an income maintenance center, you are interviewing a client to    18.____
determine his elibility for a work program. Suddenly the client begins to shout that he is in
no condition to work and that you are persecuting him for no reason.
Of the following, your *BEST* response to this client is to

    A. advise the client to stop shouting or you will call for the security guard
    B. wait until the client calms down, then order him to come back for another interview
    C. insist that you are not persecuting the client and that he must complete the inter-
       view
    D. wait until the client calms down, say that you understand how he feels, and try to
       continue the interview

19. You are counseling a mother whose 17-year-old son has recently been returned home    19.____
from a mental institution. Although she is willing to care for her son at home, she is fright-
ened by his strange and sometimes violent behavior and does not know the best
arrangement to make for his care.
Of the following, your *MOST* appropriate response to this mother's problem is to

    A. describe the supportive services and alternatives to home care which are available
    B. help her to accept her son's strange and violent behavior
    C. tell her that she will not be permitted to care for her son at home if she is frightened
       by his behavior
    D. convince her that she is not responsible for her son's mental condition

20. Assume that, as an intake worker, you are interviewing an elderly man who comes to the    20.____
center several times a month to discuss topics with you which are not related to social
services. You realize that the man is lonely and enjoys these conversations.
Of the following, it would be *MOST* appropriate to

    A. politely discourage the man from coming in to pass the time with you
    B. avoid speaking to this man the next time he comes into the center
    C. explore with the client his feelings about joining a Senior Citizens' Center
    D. continue to hold these conversations with the man

21. A client you are interviewing in the housing elibility section tends to ramble on after each    21.____
response that he gives, so that many clients are kept waiting.
In this situation, of the following, it would be *MOST* advisable to

    A. try to direct the interview, in order to obtain the necessary information
    B. reduce the number of questions asked so that you can shorten the interview
    C. arrange a second interview for the client so that you can give him more time
    D. tell the client that he is wasting everybody's time

22. A non-minority worker in an employment eligibility unit is about to interview a minority cli-    22.___
ent on public assistance for job placement when the client says: *What does your kind
know about my problems? You've never had to survive out on these streets.* Of the following, the worker's MOST appropriate response in this situation is to

    A. postpone the interview until a minority worker is available to interview the client
    B. tell the client that he must cooperate with the worker if he wants to continue receiv-
       ing public assistance
    C. explain to the client the function of the worker in this unit and the services he pro-
       vides
    D. assure the client that you do not have to be a member of a minority group to under-
       stand the effects of poverty

23. As a worker in a family services unit, you have been assigned to follow-up a case folder    23.___
recently forwarded from the protective-diagnostic unit. After making appropriate clerical
notations in your records such as name of client and date of receipt, which of the following would be the MOST appropriate step to take *next*?

    A. Confer with your supervisor
    B. Read and review all reports included in the case folder
    C. Arrange to visit with the client at his home
    D. Confer with representatives of any other agencies which have been in contact with
       the client

24. As a worker in the employment section, you are interviewing a young client who seriously    24.___
underestimates the amount of education and training he will require for a certain occupation. For you to tell the client that you think he is mistaken would, generally, be considered

    A. *inadvisable,* because workers should not express their opinions to clients
    B. *inadvisable,* because clients have the right to self-determination
    C. *advisable,* because clients should generally be alerted to their misconceptions
    D. *advisable,* because workers should convince clients to adopt a proper life style

25. As an intake worker, you are counseling a mother and her unmarried, thirteen-year-old    25.___
daughter, who is six months pregnant, concerning the advisability of placing the daughter's baby for adoption. The mother insists on adoption, but the daughter remains silent
and appears undecided. Of the following, you should encourage the daughter to

    A. make the final decision on adoption herself
    B. keep her baby despite her mother's insistence on adoption
    C. accept her mother's insistence on adoption
    D. make the decision on adoption together with her mother

# KEY (CORRECT ANSWERS)

| | | | |
|---|---|---|---|
| 1. | C | 11. | A |
| 2. | D | 12. | C |
| 3. | B | 13. | B |
| 4. | A | 14. | B |
| 5. | B | 15. | D |
| 6. | A | 16. | B |
| 7. | C | 17. | A |
| 8. | A | 18. | D |
| 9. | C | 19. | A |
| 10. | D | 20. | C |

21. A
22. C
23. B
24. C
25. D

# TEST 2

DIRECTIONS: Each question or incomplete statement is followed by several suggested answers or completions. Select the one that *BEST* answers the question or completes the statement. *PRINT THE LETTER OF THE CORRECT ANSWER IN THE SPACE AT THE RIGHT.*

1. You are interviewing a legally responsible absent father who refuses to make child support payments because he claims the mother physically abuses the child. Of the following, the *BEST* way for you to handle this situation is to tell the father that you

    A. will report his complaint about the mother, but he is still responsible for making child support payments
    B. suspect that he is complaining about the mother in order to avoid his own responsibility for making child support payments
    C. are concerned with his responsibility to make child support payments, not with the mother's abuse of the child
    D. can not determine his responsibility for making child support payments until his complaint about the mother is investigated

1.___

2. On a visit to a home where child abuse is alleged, you find the mother preparing lunch for her two children. She tells you that she knows that a neighbor is spreading lies about her treatment of the children.
Which one of the following is the *BEST* action for you to take?

    A. Thank the mother for her assistance, leave the home, and indicate in your report that the allegation of child abuse is false
    B. Tell the mother that, since you have been sent to visit her, there must be some truth to the allegations
    C. Explain the purpose of your visit and observe whatever interaction takes place between the children and the mother
    D. Conclude the interview, since you have observed the mother preparing a good lunch for the children

2.___

3. You are interviewing an elderly woman who lives alone to determine her eligibility for homemaker service at public expense. Though obviously frail and in need of this service, the woman is not completely cooperative, and,during the interview, is often silent for a considerable period of time.
Of the following, the *BEST* way for you to deal with these periods of silence is to

    A. realize that she may be embarrassed to have to apply for homemaker service at public expense, and emphasize her right to this service
    B. postpone the interview and make an appointment with her for a later date, when she may be better able to cooperate
    C. explain to the woman that you have many clients to interview and need her cooperation to complete the interview quickly
    D. recognize that she is probably hiding something and begin to ask questions to draw her out

3.___

4. During a conference with an adolescent boy at a juvenile detention center, you find out     4.\_\_\_\_
   for the first time that he would prefer to be placed in foster care rather than return to his
   natural parents.
   To uncover the reasons why the boy dislikes his own home, of the following, it would be
   *MOST* advisable for you to

   A. ask the boy a number of short, simple questions about his feelings
   B. encourage the boy to talk freely and express his feelings as best he can
   C. interview the parents and find out why the boy doesn't want to live at home
   D. administer a battery of psychological tests in order to make an assessment of the
   boy's problems

5. Of the following, the *BEST* way to determine which activities should be provided for     5.\_\_\_\_
   members of a Senior Citizens' Center is to

   A. ask the neighborhood community board to submit their recommendations
   B. meet with the professional staff of the center to get their opinions
   C. encourage the members of the center to express their personal preferences
   D. study the schedules prepared by other Senior Citizens' Centers for guidance

6. You are interviewing a mother who is applying for Aid to Families with Dependent Chil-     6.\_\_\_\_
   dren because the husband has deserted the family. The mother becomes annoyed at
   having to answer your questions and tells you to leave her apartment. Which one of the
   following actions would be *most appropriate* to take *FIRST* in this situation?

   A. Return to the office and close the case for lack of cooperation
   B. Tell the mother that you will get the information from her neighbors if she does not
   cooperate
   C. Tell the mother that you must stay until you get answers to your questions
   D. Explain to the mother the reasons for the interview and the consequences of her
   failure to cooperate

7. A worker assigned to visit homebound clients to determine their eligibility for Medicaid     7.\_\_\_\_
   must understand each client's situation as completely as possible.
   Of the following sources which may provide insight into the client's situation, the *one*
   that is generally *MOST* revealing is:

   A. Close relatives of the client, who have known him for many years
   B. Next-door neighbors, who have observed the daily living habits of the client
   C. The client himself, who can provide his own description of his situation
   D. The records of other social service agencies that may have served the client

8. A worker counseling juvenile clients finds that, although he can tolerate most of their behavior, he becomes infuriated when they lie to him.
Of the following, the worker can *BEST* deal with his anger at his clients' lying by

    A. recognizing his feelings of anger and learning to control expression of these feelings to his clients
    B. warning his clients that he cannot be responsible for his anger when a client lies to him
    C. using will power to suppress his feelings of anger when a client lies to him
    D. realizing that lying is a common trait of juveniles and not directed against him personally

8.____

9. During an interview at the employment eligibility section, one of your clients, a former drug addict, has expressed an interest in attending a community counseling center and resuming his education.
In this case, the *most appropriate* action that you should take *FIRST* is to

    A. determine whether this ambition is realistic for a former drug addict
    B. send the client's application to a community counseling center which provides services to former addicts
    C. ask the client whether he is really motivated or is just seeking your approval
    D. encourage and assist the client to take this step, since his interest is a positive sign

9.____

10. Because of habitual neglect by his mother, a five-year-old boy has been placed in a foster home.
For the worker to encourage the mother to visit the boy in the foster home is, generally,

    A. *desirable,* because the boy will be helped by continuing his ties with his mother during the separation
    B. *undesirable,* because the boy will be upset by his mother's visits and will have a harder time adjusting to the foster home
    C. *desirable,* because the mother will learn from the foster parents how she should treat the boy
    D. *undesirable,* because the mother should be punished for her neglect of the boy by complete separation from him

10.____

11. You are interviewing a client who, during previous appointments, has not responded to your requests for information required to determine his continued eligibility for services.
On this occasion, the client again offers an excuse which you feel is not acceptable.
For you to advise the client of the probable loss of services because of his lack of cooperation is

    A. *inappropriate,* because the threat to withhold services will harm the relationship between worker and client
    B. *inappropriate,* because workers should not reveal to clients that they do not believe their statements
    C. *appropriate,* because social services are a reward given to cooperative clients
    D. *appropriate,* because the worker should inform clients of the consequences of their lack of cooperation

11.____

12. Assume that you are counseling an adolescent boy in a juvenile detention center who has been a ringleader in smuggling *pot* into the center.
During your regular interview with this boy, of the following, it would be *advisable* to

    A. tell him you know that he has been involved in smuggling pot and that you are trying to understand the reasons for his misbehavior
    B. ignore his pot smuggling in order to reassure him that you understand and accept him, even though you do not agree with his standards of behavior
    C. warn him that you have reported his pot smuggling and that he will be punished for his misbehavior
    D. show him that you disapprove of his pot smuggling, but assure him that you will not report him for his misbehavior

12.____

13. Your unit has received several complaints about a homeless elderly woman living outdoors in various locations in the area. To help determine the need for protective services for this woman, you interview several persons in the neighborhood who are familiar with her, but all are uncooperative or reluctant to give information.
Of the following, your *BEST* approach to these persons is to explain to them that

    A. you will take legal steps against them if they do not cooperate with you
    B. their cooperation may enable you to help this homeless woman
    C. you need their cooperation to remove this homeless woman from their neighborhood
    D. they will be responsible for any harm that comes to this homeless woman

13.____

14. A foster mother complains to the worker that a ten-year-old boy placed with her is over-aggressive and unmanageable. The worker, knowing that the boy has been placed unsuccessfully several times before, constantly reassures the foster mother that the boy is improving steadily.
For the worker to do this is, generally,

    A. *good practice,* because the foster mother may accept the professional opinion of the worker and keep the boy
    B. *poor practice,* because the foster mother may be discouraged from discussing the boy's problems with the worker
    C. *good practice,* because the foster mother may feel guilty if she gives up the boy when he is improving
    D. *poor practice,* because the boy should not remain with a foster mother who complains about his behavior

14.____

15. Assume that, as a worker in the liaison and adjustment unit, you are interviewing a client regarding an adjustment in budget. The client begins to scream at you that she holds you responsible for the decrease in her allowance. Of the following, which is the *BEST* way for you to handle this situation?

    A. Attempt to discuss the matter calmly with the client and explain her right to a hearing
    B. Urge the client to appeal and assure her of your support
    C. Tell the client that her disorderly behavior will be held against her
    D. Tell the client that the reduction is *due to red tape* and is not your fault

15.____

16. As a worker assigned to a juvenile detention center, you are having a counseling inter-     16.\_\_\_\_
    view with a recently admitted boy who is having serious problems in adjusting to confine-
    ment in the center. During the interview, the boy frequently interrupts to ask you personal
    questions.
    Of the following, the *BEST* way for you to deal with these questions is to

    A. tell him in a friendly way that your job is to discuss his problems, not yours
    B. try to understand how the questions relate to the boy's own problems and reply
       with discretion
    C. take no notice of the questions and continue with the interview
    D. try to win the boy's confidence by answering his questions in detail

17. A worker is interviewing an elderly woman who hesitates to provide necessary informa-     17.\_\_\_\_
    tion about her finances to determine whether she is eligible for supplementary assis-
    tance. She fears that this information will be reported to others and that her neighbors
    will find out that she is destitute and applying for *welfare*.
    Of the following, the worker's *MOST* appropriate response is to

    A. tell her that, if she hesitates to give this information, the agency will get it from
       other sources
    B. assure her that this information is kept strictly confidential and will not be given to
       unauthorized persons
    C. convince her that her application will be turned down unless she provides this infor-
       mation as soon as possible
    D. ask for the name and address of her nearest relative and obtain the information
       from that person

18. You are counseling a couple whose children have been placed in a foster home because     18.\_\_\_\_
    of the couple's quarreling and child neglect. When you interview the wife by herself, she
    tells you that she knows the husband often *cheats* on her with other women, but she is
    too afraid of the husband's temper to tell him how much this hurts her. For you to imme-
    diately reveal to the husband the wife's unhappiness concerning his *cheating* is, gener-
    ally,

    A. *good practice,* because it will help the husband to understand why his wife quarrels
       with him
    B. *poor practice,* because information received from the wife should not be given to
       the husband without her permission
    C. *good practice,* because the husband will direct his anger at you rather than at his
       wife
    D. *poor practice,* because the wife may have told you a false story about her husband
       in order to win your sympathy

19. A worker in an employment eligibility section is beginning a job placement interview with    19.____
a tall, strongly-built young man. As the man sits down, the worker comments: *I know a
big fellow like you wouldn't be interested in any clerical job.*
For the worker to make such a comment is, generally,

    A. *appropriate,* because it creates an air of familiarity which may put the man at ease
    B. *inappropriate,* because the man may be sensitive about his physical size
    C. *appropriate,* because the worker is using his judgment to help speed up the inter-
view
    D. *inappropriate,* because the man may feel he is being pressured into agreeing with
the worker

20. Workers at a juvenile detention center are responsible for establishing constructive rela-    20.____
tionships with the youths confined to the center in order to help them adjust to detention.
Of the following, the *BEST* way for a worker to deal with a youth who acts over-aggressive and hostile is to

    A. take appropriate disciplinary measures
    B. attempt to distract the youth by encouraging him to engage in physical sports
    C. try to discover the real reasons for the youth's hostile behavior
    D. urge the youth to express his anger against the institution instead of *taking it out* on
you

21. A worker in a men's shelter is counseling a middle-aged client for alcoholism. During    21.____
counseling, the client confesses that, many years ago, he had often enjoyed sexually
abusing his ten-year-old daughter. The worker tells the client that he personally finds the
client's behavior *morally disgusting.* For the worker to tell the client this is, generally,

    A. *acceptable counseling practice,* because it may encourage the client to feel guilty
about his behavior
    B. *unacceptable counseling practice,* because the client may try to shock the worker
by confessing other similar behavior
    C. *acceptable counseling practice,* because *letting off steam* in this manner may
relieve tension between the worker and the client
    D. *unacceptable counseling practice,* because the client may hesitate to discuss his
behavior frankly with the worker in the future

22. During your discussion with a foster mother who has had a nine-year-old boy in place-    22.____
ment for about one month, you are told that the child is disruptive in school and has been
unruly and hostile toward the foster family. The boy had been quiet and docile before
placement.
In this situation, it would be *MOST* appropriate to suggest to the foster mother that

    A. this behavior is normal for a nine-year-old boy
    B. children placed in foster homes usually go through a period of testing their foster
parents
    C. the child must have picked up these patterns from the foster family
    D. this behavior is probably a sign that she is too strict with the boy

23. During an interview in the housing eligibility section, your client, who wants to move to a    23.____
larger apartment, asks you to decide on a suitable neighborhood for her. For you, the
worker, to make such a decision for the client would generally be considered

    A. *appropriate,* because you can save time and expense by sharing your knowledge
       of neighborhoods with the client
    B. *inappropriate,* because workers should not help clients with this type of decision
    C. *appropriate,* because this will help the client to develop confidence in her ability to
       make decisions
    D. *inappropriate* because the client should be encouraged to accept the responsibility
       of making this decision

24. Your client, an elderly man left unable to care for himself after a stroke, has been referred    24.____
for home-attendant services, but insists that he does not need these services. You
believe that the man considers this to be an insult to his pride and that he will not allow
himself to admit that he needs help.
Of the following, the *MOST* appropriate action for you to take is to

    A. withdraw the referral for home-attendant services and allow the client to try to take
       care of himself
    B. process the request for home-attendant services on the assumption that the client
       will soon realize that he cannot care for himself
    C. discuss with the client your interpretation of his problem and attempt to persuade
       him to accept home-attendant services
    D. tell the client that he will have no further opportunity to apply for home-attendant
       services if he does not accept them at this time

25. A worker making a field visit to investigate a complaint of child abuse finds that the par-    25.____
ents of the child are a racially mixed couple. The child appears poorly dressed and
unruly.
Of the following, the *MOST* appropriate approach for the worker to take in this situation
is to

    A. take the child aside and ask him privately if either of his parents ever mistreats him
    B. determine if prejudice against the couple has led them to use the child as a scape-
       goat
    C. question the non-minority parent closely for signs of resentment of the child's
       mixed parentage
    D. observe the relationship between parents and child for indications of abuse by the
       parents

# KEY (CORRECT ANSWERS)

| | | | | |
|---|---|---|---|---|
| 1. | A | | 11. | D |
| 2. | C | | 12. | A |
| 3. | A | | 13. | B |
| 4. | B | | 14. | B |
| 5. | C | | 15. | A |
| 6. | D | | 16. | B |
| 7. | C | | 17. | B |
| 8. | A | | 18. | B |
| 9. | D | | 19. | D |
| 10. | A | | 20. | C |

| | |
|---|---|
| 21. | D |
| 22. | B |
| 23. | D |
| 24. | C |
| 25. | D |

# EXAMINATION SECTION
## TEST 1

DIRECTIONS: Each question or incomplete statement is followed by several suggested answers or completions. Select the one that *BEST* answers the question or completes the statement. *PRINT THE LETTER OF THE CORRECT ANSWER IN THE SPACE AT THE RIGHT.*

1. A client tells you that he is extremely upset by the treatment that he received from Center personnel at the information desk.
Which of the following is the *BEST* way to handle this complaint during the interview?

   A. Explain to the client that he probably misinterpreted what occurred at the information desk
   B. Let the client express his feelings and then proceed with the interview
   C. Tell the client that you are not concerned with the personnel at the information desk
   D. Escort the client to the information desk to find out what really happened

1.____

2. As a worker in the foster home division, you are reviewing a case record to determine whether a 13-year-old boy, in foster care because of neglect and mistreatment by his natural parents, should be returned home. The natural parents, who want to take the child back, have been in family counseling, with encouraging results, and have improved their living conditions.
Of the following, it would be appropriate to recommend that the child

   A. remain with the foster parents, since this is a documented case of child abuse
   B. remain with the foster parents until they are ready to send him home
   C. be returned to his natural parents, since they have made positive efforts to change their behavior toward the child
   D. be returned to his natural parents, because continued separation will cause irreparable damage to the child

2.____

3. You are finishing an interview with a client in which you have explained to her the procedure she must go through to apply for income maintenance.
Of the following, the *BEST* way for you to make sure that she has fully understood the procedure is to ask her

   A. whether she feels she has understood your explanation of the procedure
   B. whether she has any questions to ask you about the procedure
   C. to describe the procedure to you in her own words
   D. a few questions to test her understanding of the procedure

3.____

4. Mrs. Carey, a widow with five children, has come to the field office to seek foster care for her 13-year-old daughter, who has often been truant from school and has recently been caught shoplifting. Mrs. Carey says that she cannot maintain a proper home environment for the other four children and deal with her daughter at the same time.
Of the following, you should *FIRST*

   A. process Mrs. Carey's request for placement of her daughter in a foster care agency
   B. interview both Mrs. Carey and her daughter to get a more complete picture of the situation
   C. suggest to Mrs. Carey that she might be able to manage if she obtained homemaker services
   D. warn the daughter that she will be sent away from home if she does not change her behavior

4.____

5. During a group orientation meeting with couples who wish to adopt babies through your agency, one couple asks you how they should deal with the question of whether the child should be told that he is adopted.
Of the following, your *BEST* response to this couple is to

    A. tell them to conceal from the child the fact that he is adopted
    B. suggest that they lead the child to believe that his natural parents are dead
    C. tell them to inform the child that they know nothing about his natural parents
    D. explore with them their feelings about revealing to the child that he is adopted

5.____

6. You are beginning an investigation of an anonymous complaint that a welfare client has a concealed bank account. Of the following, the *FIRST* step you should generally take in conducting this investigation is to

    A. confront the client with the complaint during an office interview
    B. try to track down the source of the anonymous complaint
    C. make a surprise visit to the client in his home to question him
    D. gather any available information from bank and agency records

6.____

7. When investigating the location of an absent parent, the worker frequently interviews the parent's friends and neighbors. The worker often writes down the information given by the person interviewed and, at the end of the interview, summarizes the information to the person.
For the worker to do this is, generally,

    A. *good practice,* because the person interviewed will be Impressed by the efficiency of the worker
    B. *poor practice,* because the person interviewed may become impatient with the worker for repeating the information
    C. *good practice,* because the person interviewed has an opportunity to correct any errors the worker may have in recording the information
    D. *poor practice,* because summarizing the information may encourage the person to waste time adding and changing information

7.____

8. During an interview for the purpose of investigating a charge of child abuse, a client first denied that she had abused her child, but then burst into tears and promised that she *will never do it again.*
Of the following, the *MOST* appropriate action for the worker to take in this situation is to

    A. tell the client that, since she has already lied, it is difficult to believe that she will keep her promise
    B. show a concern for the client's feelings but tell her that you will have to report your findings and refer her for help
    C. determine the extent to which the child was abused and close the case if no permanent harm was done
    D. explain to the client that she has already done enough harm to the child and you must, therefore, recommend placement

8.____

9. As a worker involved in locating absent parents, you have obtained information indicating that the address for the putative father is the same as the client's address. In order to determine whether, in fact, the client and putative father are living together, of the following, it would be *MOST* appropriate to

9.____

A. visit the address and question the neighbors and superintendent about the putative father
B. visit the client to ask her why she has concealed the fact that the putative father is living with her
C. file the information in the case folder and wait for confirming information
D. close the client's case and issue a recoupment notice to the putative father

10. A client claims that she never received a welfare check that was due her. As part of your investigation of her claim, you obtain from the bank a copy of the check, which has been endorsed with her name and cashed.
Of the following, the *BEST* procedure for you to follow in this investigation is to

    10.____

A. end the investigation immediately, since the client's claim cannot be proved
B. interview the client and show her the copy of the cashed check
C. tell the client that you have evidence that her claim is false
D. say nothing about the cashed check and try to trap the client in a false statement

11. As part of the investigation to locate an absent father, you make a field visit to interview one of the father's friends. Before beginning the interview, you identify yourself to the friend and show him your official identification.
For you to do this is, generally,

    11.____

A. *good practice,* because the friend will have proof that you are authorized to make such confidential investigations
B. *poor practice,* because the friend may not answer your questions when he knows why you are interviewing him
C. *good practice,* because your supervisor can confirm from the friend that you actually made the interview
D. *poor practice,* because the friend may warn the absent father that your agency is looking for him

12. As a field office worker you are investigating a citizen's complaint charging a mother of three children with child neglect. The mother tells you that her husband has become depressed after losing his job and is often abusive to her, and that this situation has made her feel anxious and has made it difficult for her to care for the children properly.
*Which one* of the following is the *BEST* way for you to respond to this situation?

    12.____

A. Tell the mother that she must do everything possible to help her husband find a job
B. Arrange to meet the husband so you can explain to him the consequences of his behavior
C. Investigate the complaint, report your findings, and refer the family for counseling or other appropriate services
D. Suggest that the family obtain homemaker services so that the mother can go to work

13. You are interviewing a client in his home as part of your investigation of an anonymous complaint that he has been receiving Medicaid fraudulently. During the interview, the client frequently interrupts your questions to discuss the hardships of his life and the bitterness he feels about his medical condition.
Of the following, the *BEST* way for you to deal with these discussions is to

    13.____

A. cut them off abruptly, since the client is probably just trying to avoid answering your questions

B.   listen patiently, since these discussions may be helpful to the client and may give you information for your investigation
C.   remind the client that you are investigating a complaint against him and he must answer directly
D.   seek to gain the client's confidence by discussing any personal or medical problems which you yourself may have

14.   While interviewing an absent father to determine his ability to pay child support, you realize that his answers to some of your questions contradict his answers to other questions. Of the following, the BEST way for you to try to get accurate information from the father is to                                                                                                         14._____

A.   confront him with his contradictory answers and demand an explanation from him
B.   use your best judgment as to which of his answers are accurate and question him accordingly
C.   tell him that he has misunderstood your questions and that he must clarify his answers
D.   ask him the same questions in different words and follow up his answers with related questions

15.   You are assigned to investigate a complaint of child neglect made against a minority mother by her non-minority neighbor. During an interview with you, the neighbor states that the mother allows her children to run around the streets half-dressed till late at night, and adds: *Of course, what can you expect from any of those people anyway?* Of the following, your MOST appropriate action is to                                          15._____

A.   end the investigation, since the neighbor is clearly too prejudiced to be reliable
B.   tell the mother that the neighbor has made a complaint of child neglect against her
C.   seek evidence to support the complaint of child neglect made by the neighbor
D.   continue the interview with the neighbor in an attempt to get at the root of his prejudice against the mother

16.   You are interviewing a couple with regard to available services for the husband's aged mother. During the interview, the husband casually mentions that he and his wife are thinking about becoming foster parents and would like to get some information on foster care programs offered through the department of social services. Of the following agencies within social services, the MOST appropriate one for you to refer this couple to is                                                                                        16._____

A.   family and adult services
B.   special services for children
C.   bureau of child support
D.   special services for adults

17.   You have been helping one of your clients to obtain medical assistance for her two young children. Accidentally, you obtain evidence that the client may be involved in a criminal scheme to collect duplicate welfare checks at several different addresses. Of the following offices of the department of social services, the MOST appropriate one to which you should report this evidence is                                                                            17._____
A.   the inspector general
B.   case intake and management
C.   the general counsel
D.   income support

Questions 18-25.

DIRECTIONS:   Questions 18 through 25 are to be answered *SOLELY* on the basis of the FACT SITUATION and REPORT FORM.

## FACT SITUATION

On June 5, 2013, Mary Adams (Case No. ADC-2095732), lining at 1507 Montague Street, Apt. 3C, Brooklyn, New York, applied and was accepted for public assistance for herself and her three dependant children. Her husband, John, had left their home after an argument the previous week and had not returned, leaving Mrs. Adams without funds of any kind. She had tried to contact him at his place of employment, but was told that he had resigned several days prior to her call. When the Case Worker questioned Mrs. Adams about her husband's employment, income, and bank accounts, Mrs. Adams stated that he had done carpentry work during most of the years he had worked; his last known employer had been the Avco Lumber Company, 309 Amber Street, Queens, New York, where he had earned a weekly salary of $300. She then showed the Case Worker two bankbooks in her husband's name, which indicated a balance of $500 in one account and $275 in the other. A visit to Mr. Brown, a neighbor of the Adams', by the Case Worker, revealed that Mr. Adams had also told Mr. Brown about the existence of the bankbooks. A visit to the Avco Lumber Company by the Case Worker confirmed that Mr. Adams' gross salary had been $300 a week. This visit also revealed that Mr. Adams was a member of the Woodworkers' Union, Local #7, and that Mr. Adams' previous home address for the period from February '02 to June '08 was 1109 Wellington Street, Brooklyn, New York.

| REPORT FORM | |
|---|---|
| A.  **CLIENT:** | |
| 1. Name:_____ | |
| 2. Address: _____ | |
| 3. Case No.: _____ | |
| 4. Acceptance Date:_____ | |
| 5. No. of Dependent Children: _____ | |
| B.  **ABSENT PARENT:** | |
| 1. Name:_____ | |
| 2. Date of birth _____ | |
| 3. Place of Birth:_____ | |
| 4. Present Address: _____ | |
| 5. Regular Occupation: _____ | |
| 6. Union Affiliation: _____ | |
| 7. Name of Last Employer:_____ | |
| 8. Address of Last Employer: _____ | |
| 9.   a.   Weekly Earnings (Gross):_____ | |
|       b.   How Verified:_____ | |
| 10.   a.   Weekly Earnings (Net):   _____ | |
|       b.   How Verified:_____ | |
| 11.   a.   Amount of Bank Accounts:_____ | |
|       b.   How Verified:_____ | |
| 12. Social Security No.:_____ | |
| 13. Last Known Home Address: _____ | |
| 14. Previous Addresses:_____ | |

18. Based on the information given in the FACT SITUATION, the *MOST* appropriate of the following entries for item B.II.b is:      18.____

   A. *Revealed to Case Worker by Mrs. Adams*
   B. *Confirmed by visit to Mr. Brown*
   C. *Revealed by Woodworkers' Union, Local #7*
   D. *Confirmed by bankbooks shown by Mrs. Adams*

19. The *one* of the following which *BEST* answers item B.4 is:      19.____

   A. *unknown*
   B. *c/o Avco Lumber Company*
   C. *1109 Wellington Street, Brooklyn, New York*
   D. *1507 Montague Street, Brooklyn, New York*

20. Based on the information given in the FACT SITUATION, it is *NOT* possible to answer item      20.____

   A.  A.2          B.  A.5          C.  B.6          D.  B.10

21. The *one* of the following which would be *LEAST* helpful in tracing the missing parent is information found in item      21.____

   A.  B.12          B.  B.10.a          C.  B.6          D.  B.1

22. Based on the information given in the FACT SITUATION, it is *most likely* that the *SAME* entry would be made for items      22.____

   A.  A.1 and B.1              B.  A.4 and B.2
   C.  B.9.a and B.10.a         D.  A.2 and B.13

23. Based on the information in the FACT SITUATION, the entry : *1109 Wellington Street, Brooklyn, New York* would *most likely* be placed for item      23.____

   A.  A.2          B.  B.4          C.  B.8          D.  B.14

24. The *one* of the following items that can be answered based on the information given in the FACT SITUATION is      24.____

   A.  B.2          B.  B.3          C.  B.9.b          D.  B.12

25. Based on the information given in the FACT SITUATION, the figure *775* would appear in the entry for      25.____

   A.  A.3          B.  B.12          C.  B.9.a          D.  B.11.a

# KEY (CORRECT ANSWERS)

| | | | | |
|---|---|---|---|---|
| 1. | B | | 11. | A |
| 2. | C | | 12. | C |
| 3. | C | | 13. | B |
| 4. | B | | 14. | D |
| 5. | D | | 15. | C |
| 6. | D | | 16. | B |
| 7. | C | | 17. | A |
| 8. | B | | 18. | D |
| 9. | A | | 19. | A |
| 10. | B | | 20. | D |

| | |
|---|---|
| 21. | B |
| 22. | D |
| 23. | D |
| 24. | C |
| 25. | D |

# TEST 2

DIRECTIONS:   Each question or incomplete statement is followed by several suggested answers or completions. Select the one that BEST answers the question or completes the statement. *PRINT THE LETTER OF THE CORRECT ANSWER IN THE SPACE AT THE RIGHT.*

1.  A worker in a senior adult center is approached by one of his clients, an elderly man living alone and suffering from severe arthritis, who asks him how to go about obtaining homemaker services through the department of social services.
    Of the following, the *MOST* appropriate office of the department to which the worker should refer this client is:

    A.   income support
    B.   protective services for adults
    C.   income maintenance
    D.   case intake and management

1.___

2.  Workers assigned to locate absent parents frequently ask various governmental agencies to search their records for information useful in determining the address of the person they are seeking.
    Of the following, the agency which is likely to be useful *most frequently* for this purpose is the

    A.   motor vehicle bureau
    B.   office of the district attorney
    C.   department of investigation
    D.   health and hospitals corporation

2.___

Questions 3-7.

DIRECTIONS:   Questions 3 through 7 are to be answered *SOLELY* on the basis of the FACT SITUATION and PRELIMINARY INVESTIGATION FORM.

## FACT SITUATION

COMPLAINT:

On March 1, Mrs. Mona Willard, a neighbor of the Smith family, reported to the Police Department that the Smith children, were being severely neglected, and she requested that an investigation be conducted. She based her complaint on the fact that, since the time three weeks ago when Janet Smith's husband, Charles, deserted Mrs. Smith and their two children, John, age 2, and Darlene, age 4, the children have been seen wandering in the neighborhood at all hours, inadequately dressed against the cold.

INVESTIGATION:

Investigation by the Police Department and the Department of Social Services revealed that the above charge was true and, further, that Mrs. Smith had inflicted cruel and harsh physical treatment upon the children in an attempt to discipline them. The children were immediately removed from their parent' s care and placed in a medical facility for tests and observation. It as found that the children were suffering from serious malnutrition and anemia and that they also showed signs of emotional disturbance.

## CASE ACTION DECISION:

Conferences which you, the Case Worker, have held with Dr. Charles Jordan, a physician treating Mrs. Smith, and with Ellen Farraday, a psychiatric social worker from the Mental Health Consultation Center, confirm that Mrs. Smith is emotionally unstable at the present time and cannot care for her children. A written report from the Chief Resident Physician at the hospital where the children have been placed indicates that both children are presently doing well, but when released will need the security of an emotionally stable atmosphere. It has therefore been decided that placement in a foster he ia necessary for the children until such time as Mrs. Smith is judged to be capable of caring for them.

---

### PRELIMINARY INVESTIGATION FORM

1. Child(ren) in Need of Protection :
   - a. Name(s): _____
   - b. Age (s) : _____

2. Alleged Perpetrator :
   - a. Name: _____
   - b. Relationship: _____

3. Present Status of Child(ren):
   - ☐ a. Remaining with Subject Pending Investigation
   - ☐ b. Removed to Relatives
   - ☐ c. Removed to Foster Care
   - ☐ d. In Hospital
   - ☐ e. Other

4. Actions or Services Needed for Child(ren):
   - ☐ a. Housekeeper
   - ☐ b. Homemaker
   - ☐ c. Day Care
   - ☐ d. Home Attendant
   - ☐ e. Relatives
   - ☐ f. Foster Care

5. Contacts Made to Support Case Action Decision:

| | I<br>Phone | II<br>Personal | III<br>Written |
|---|---|---|---|
| a. Medical; School | ☐ | ☐ | ☐ |
| b. Relatives | ☐ | ☐ | ☐ |
| c. Social Agency | ☐ | ☐ | ☐ |
| d. Other | ☐ | ☐ | ☐ |

3. The *one* of the following that should be entered in space 2.b is          3.___

    A. mother        B. father        C. neighbor        D. physician

4. The *one* of the following boxes that should be checked in item 3 is          4.___

    A. a        B. c        C. d        D. e

5. The *one* of the following boxes that should be checked in item 4 is          5.___

    A. a        B. c        C. d        D. f

6. Based on the information given in the FACT SITUATION, the boxes that should be          6.___
checked off in item 5 are:

    A. a-II, a-III, c-II                B. a-II, c-II, c-III
    C. a-I, a-II, a-III                D. b-II, c-I, c-II

7. The *one* of the following that would *CORRECTLY* appear as part of the entry to item 1.a          7.___
is

    A. Mona        B. Janet        C. Darlene        D. Ellen

Questions 8-12.

DIRECTIONS:   Answer Questions 8 through 12 *SOLELY* on the basis of the information contained in the following passage:

It is desirable, whenever possible, to have long-term elderly patients return to their own
homes after hospitalization, provided that the medical condition is not acute. Of course, there
must be room for the patient; the family must be able to provide some necessary care; and a
physician's services must be available. Although the patient's family may be able to provide
most services for the patient in his own home, this is generally unlikely because of the nature
of the illness and the patient's need for a variety of services. Recently, hospital personnel,
public health workers, visiting nurse associations, and community leaders have been
developing home-care programs, which make the services of the hospital available to the
patient who is not ill enough to require the concentrated technical facilities of a general hospital, but who is unable to attend an outpatient clinic or a physician's office. These services are
those of the physician, visiting nurse, physical therapist, occupational therapist, social worker,
and homemaker, as needed. There is also provision for readmission to the hospital for specific purposes and return to home care.

8. According to the passage above, it would be *UNDESIRABLE* to have an elderly patient          8.___
return to his own home after hospitalization when the patient

    A. requires the services of a doctor
    B. may be in immediate danger due to his medical condition
    C. is under physical or occupational therapy
    D. cannot go to the outpatient clinic of the hospital

9. According to the passage above, the *services of the hospital* which are made available          9.___
by home-care programs include those of

    A. dietitians                 B. visiting nurses
    C. public health administrators    D. community workers

10. The *one* of the following statements about home-care programs which is *BEST* supported by the paragraph above is that home-care programs
    A. have been developed in part by hospital personnel
    B. relieve workloads of hospital personnel
    C. decrease public expenditures for hospitalization of the elderly
    D. reduce readmissions of elderly patients to hospitals

10.____

11. According to the above passage, home-care programs would be *LEAST* likely to include the services of a
    A. homemaker              B. social worker
    C. physician               D. hospital technician

11.____

12. It may be *inferred* from the passage above that a *MAJOR* purpose of home-care programs is to
    A. increase the demand for physicians, nurses, and other medical personnel
    B. provide patients in their homes with services similar to those provided in hospitals
    C. reduce the need for general hospitals and outpatient clinics
    D. relieve the family of their responsibility of caring for the patient

12.____

Questions 13-17.

DIRECTIONS: Answer Questions 13 through 17 *SOLELY* on the basis of the information contained in the following DUTIES STATEMENT.

---

### DUTIES STATEMENT OF THE VIOLATION CENTER (VC) CASE WORKER

1. Receives telephone, mail, and in-person reports of suspected violations from mandated and non-mandated sources, as well as from the New York State Violation Bureau (NYSVB). Informs mandated sources that they must send a written summary of their report, on form DSS-555, within 48 hours, to the Central Office of VC, 265 Church Street, New York, N. Y.

2. Completes in-office portion of DSS-555 received from mandated sources as fully as possible. Checks that report summary is specific, factual, and detailed. (See NYSVB Instructions on page 213.)

3. When DSS-555 is received, clears Central Office of VC for any previous record of violation on file in Central Office. If record exists, enters additional information from file record on to DSS-555. Also requests Central Office Clerk to provide appropriate record number of previous record and enters additional information from file record on to DSS-555. Also requests Central Office Clerk to provide appropriate record number of previous record and enters it in correct box on form.

4. Determines appropriate Central Office Sex Code and Reporting Source Code for each violation. (The Codes are in the VC Manual.) The codes are then entered on the bottom of the reverse side of the DSS-555.

5. Determines appropriate Service Area Code for the address in the summary. The address is the location of the violation, if known. (If the location of the violation is unknown, the address of the primary witness shall be used.) Enters Service Area Code on reverse of DSS-555. All report summaries involving violations by N.Y.C. employees are sent to the Manhattan Borough Office of VC for clearance and transmittal to BEM.

13. According to the DUTIES STATEMENT above, when a report of a suspected violation is received, a written summary of their report on DSS-555 must be sent within 48 hours by 13.__

    A. mandated sources    B. non-mandated sources  C. the NYSVB
    D. mandated and non-mandated sources, as well as by the NYSVB

14. From the above DUTIES STATEMENT, it may be *inferred* that the Case Worker whose duties are described is *most likely* assigned to 14.__

    A. the Manhattan Borough Office of VC
    B. the New York State Violation Bureau
    C. the Central Office of VC
    D. BEM

15. According to the DUTIES STATEMENT above, the Central Office Sex Code is entered on the DSS-555 15.__

    A. on the opposite side from the Service Area Code
    B. on the front of the form
    C. above the Service Area Code on the form
    D. on the bottom of the back of the form

16. According to the above DUTIES STATEMENT, a Case Worker can determine the appropriate Reporting Source Code for a violation by consulting 16.__

    A. NYSVB Instructions          B. the Central Office Clerk
    C. the VC Manual             D. the Service Area Code

17. As used in paragraph 2 of the DUTIES STATEMENT above, the word *detailed* means, most nearly, 17.__

    A. fully descriptive          B. complicated
    C. of considerable length     D. well-written

Questions 18-25.

DIRECTIONS:   Refer to the following SEMI-MONTHLY FAMILY ALLOWANCE SCHEDULE and CONVERSION TABLE when answering Questions 18 through 25.

## FIGURE NO. 1

SEMI-MONTHLY FAMILY ALLOWANCE SCHEDULE FOR MAINTENANCE OF LEGALLY RESPONSIBLE RELATIVE AND DEPENDENTS, BASED UPON
TOTAL NUMBER OF PERSONS IN PRESENT HOUSEHOLD. (ALL SURPLUS IS TO BE USED AS CONTRIBUTION TO RECIPIENTS OF PUBLIC ASSISTANCE.)

| TOTAL NUMBER OF PERSONS IN PRESENT HOUSEHOLD | ONE | TWO | THREE | FOUR | FIVE | SIX | EACH ADDITIONAL PERSON |
|---|---|---|---|---|---|---|---|
| SEMI-MONTHLY FAMILY ALLOWANCE | $1600 | $1915 | $2200 | $2605 | $2800 | $3205 | $350 |

# FIGURE NO. 2
## CONVERSION TABLE - WEEKLY TO SEMI-MONTHLY AMOUNTS

### DOLLARS

| Weekly Amount | Semi-Monthly Amount | Weekly Amount | Semi-Monthly Amount |
|---|---|---|---|
| $10.00 | $21.70 | $510.00 | $1105.00 |
| 20.00 | 43.30 | 520.00 | 1126.70 |
| 30.00 | 65.00 | 530.00 | 1148.30 |
| 40.00 | 86.70 | 540.00 | 1170.00 |
| 50.00 | 108.30 | 550.00 | 1191.70 |
| 60.00 | 130.00 | 560.00 | 1213.30 |
| 70.00 | 151.70 | 570.00 | 1235.00 |
| 80.00 | 173.30 | 580.00 | 1256.70 |
| 90.00 | 195.00 | 590.00 | 1278.30 |
| 100.00 | 216.70 | 600.00 | 1300.00 |
| 110.00 | 238.30 | 610.00 | 1321.70 |
| 120.00 | 260.00 | 620.00 | 1343.30 |
| 130.00 | 281.70 | 630.00 | 1365.00 |
| 140.00 | 303.30 | 640.00 | 1386.70 |
| 150.00 | 325.00 | 650.00 | 1408.30 |
| 160.00 | 346.70 | 660.00 | 1430.00 |
| 170.00 | 368.30 | 670.00 | 1451.70 |
| 180.00 | 390.00 | 680.00 | 1473.30 |
| 190.00 | 411.70 | 690.00 | 1495.00 |
| 200.00 | 433.30 | 700.00 | 1516.70 |
| 210.00 | 455.00 | 710.00 | 1538.30 |
| 220.00 | 476.70 | 720.00 | 1560.00 |
| 230.00 | 498.30 | 730.00 | 1581.70 |
| 240.00 | 520.00 | 740.00 | 1603.30 |
| 250.00 | 541.70 | 750.00 | 1625.00 |
| 260.00 | 563.30 | 760.00 | 1646.70 |
| 270.00 | 585.00 | 770.00 | 1668.30 |
| 280.00 | 606.70 | 780.00 | 1690.00 |
| 290.00 | 628.30 | 790.00 | 1711.70 |
| 300.00 | 650.00 | 800.00 | 1733.30 |
| 310.00 | 671.70 | 810.00 | 1755.00 |
| 320.00 | 693.30 | 820.00 | 1776.70 |
| 330.00 | 715.00 | 830.00 | 1798.30 |
| 340.00 | 736.70 | 840.00 | 1820.00 |
| 350.00 | 783.00 | 850.00 | 1841.70 |
| 360.00 | 780.00 | 860.00 | 1863.30 |
| 370.00 | 801.70 | 870.00 | 1885.00 |
| 380.00 | 823.30 | 880.00 | 1906.70 |
| 390.00 | 845.00 | 890.00 | 1928.30 |
| 400.00 | 866.70 | 900.00 | 1950.00 |
| 410.00 | 888.30 | 910.00 | 1971.70 |
| 420.00 | 910.00 | 920.00 | 1993.30 |
| 430.00 | 931.70 | 930.00 | 2015.00 |
| 440.00 | 953.30 | 940.00 | 2036.70 |
| 450.00 | 975.00 | 950.00 | 2058.30 |
| 460.00 | 996.70 | 960.00 | 2080.00 |
| 470.00 | 1018.30 | 970.00 | 2101.70 |
| 480.00 | 1040.00 | 980.00 | 2123.30 |
| 490.00 | 1061.70 | 990.00 | 2145.00 |
| 500.00 | 1083.30 | 1000.00 | 2166.70 |

### CENTS

| Weekly Amount | Semi-Monthly Amount | Weekly Amount | Semi-Monthly Amount |
|---|---|---|---|
| $0.10 | $0.20 | $5.10 | $11.10 |
| 0.20 | 0.40 | 5.20 | 11.30 |
| 0.30 | 0.70 | 5.30 | 11.50 |
| 0.40 | 0.90 | 5.40 | 11.70 |
| 0.50 | 1.10 | 5.50 | 11.90 |
| 0.60 | 1.30 | 5.60 | 12.10 |
| 0.70 | 1.50 | 5.70 | 12.40 |
| 0.80 | 1.70 | 5.80 | 12.60 |
| 0.90 | 2.00 | 5.90 | 12.80 |
| 1.00 | 2.20 | 6.00 | 13.00 |
| 1.10 | 2.40 | 6.10 | 13.20 |
| 1.20 | 2.60 | 6.20 | 13.40 |
| 1.30 | 2.80 | 6.30 | 13.70 |
| 1.40 | 3.00 | 6.40 | 13.90 |
| 1.50 | 3.30 | 6.50 | 14.10 |
| 1.60 | 3.50 | 6.60 | 14.30 |
| 1.70 | 3.70 | 6.70 | 14.50 |
| 1.80 | 3.90 | 6.80 | 14.70 |
| 1.90 | 4.10 | 6.90 | 15.00 |
| 2.00 | 4.30 | 7.00 | 15.20 |
| 2.10 | 4.60 | 7.10 | 15.40 |
| 2.20 | 4.80 | 7.20 | 15.60 |
| 2.30 | 5.00 | 7.30 | 15.80 |
| 2.40 | 5.20 | 7.40 | 16.00 |
| 2.50 | 5.40 | 7.50 | 16.30 |
| 2.60 | 5.60 | 7.60 | 16.50 |
| 2.70 | 5.90 | 7.70 | 16.70 |
| 2.80 | 6.10 | 7.80 | 16.90 |
| 2.90 | 6.30 | 7.90 | 17.10 |
| 3.00 | 6.50 | 8.00 | 17.30 |
| 3.10 | 6.70 | 8.10 | 17.60 |
| 3.20 | 6.90 | 8.20 | 17.80 |
| 3.30 | 7.20 | 8.30 | 18.00 |
| 3.40 | 7.40 | 8.40 | 18.20 |
| 3.50 | 7.60 | 8.50 | 18.40 |
| 3.60 | 7.80 | 8.60 | 18.60 |
| 3.70 | 8.00 | 8.70 | 18.90 |
| 3.80 | 8.20 | 8.80 | 19.10 |
| 3.90 | 8.50 | 8.90 | 18.30 |
| 4.00 | 8.70 | 9.00 | 19.50 |
| 4.10 | 8.90 | 9.10 | 19.70 |
| 4.20 | 9.10 | 9.20 | 19.90 |
| 4.30 | 9.30 | 9.30 | 20.20 |
| 4.40 | 9.50 | 9.40 | 20.40 |
| 4.50 | 9.80 | 9.50 | 20.60 |
| 4.60 | 10.00 | 9.60 | 20.80 |
| 4.70 | 10.20 | 9.70 | 21.00 |
| 4.80 | 10.40 | 9.80 | 21.20 |
| 4.90 | 10.60 | 9.90 | 21.50 |
| 5.00 | 10.80 | | |

DIRECTIONS: Questions 18 through 25 are to be answered *SOLELY* on the basis of the SEMI-MONTHLY FAMILY ALLOWANCE SCHEDULE FOR MAINTENANCE OF LEGALLY RESPONSIBLE RELATIVE (FIGURE NO. 1) and CONVERSION TABLE (FIGURE NO. 2) given on pages 5 and 6 and the information and case situations given below.

Questions 18 through 21 are based on Case Situation No. 1;
Questions 22 through 25 are based on Case Situation No. 2.

## INFORMATION

Legally responsible relatives living apart from persons on public assistance are asked to contribute toward the support of these persons. The amount of contribution depends on several factors, such as the number of persons in the legally responsible relative's present household who are dependent on his income (including himself), the amount of his gross income, and his expenses incident to employment. Since his contribution is computed on a semi-monthly basis, all figures must be broken down into semi-monthly amounts. Weekly amounts can be converted into semi-monthly amounts by using the conversion table on page 6.

The amount of support is computed as follows:
1. Determine total weekly gross income (the wages or salary *before* payroll deductions) of legally responsible relative.
2. Deduct all weekly expenses incident to employment such as federal, state, and city income taxes, Social Security payments, State Disability Insurance payments, union dues, cost of transportation, and $10.00 maximum per work day for lunch.
3. Remaining income shall be considered as weekly net income of legally responsible relative.
4. Convert weekly net income to semi-monthly net income, using data in FIGURE NO. 2.
5. Semi-monthly net income is compared to the semi-monthly allowance (see FIGURE NO. 1). If there is an excess of net income, then that amount is considered available as the contribution to the public assistance household. If the semi-monthly allowance is greater than the semi-monthly net income, then there is an income deficit, and there is no income available as a contribution to the public assistance household.
6. The formula for computing the semi-monthly contribution is:

Semi-Monthly Net Income
- Semi-Monthly Family Allowance
= Semi-Monthly Amount of Income Available Towards Contribution to Public Assistance Household

*Case Situation No. 1*

Mr. Andrew Young is separated from his wife and family and lives with one dependent in a 3-room furnished apartment. Mr. Young is employed as a dishwasher and his gross wages are $1000.00 per week. He is employed 5 days a week and spends $14.00 a day carfare. He spends $20.00 a work day on lunch. His weekly salary deductions are as follows:

| | |
|---|---|
| Federal Income Tax | $142.30 |
| State Income Tax | 26.00 |
| City Income Tax | 9.80 |
| Social Security | 62.10 |
| New York State Disability Insurance | 5.30 |
| Union Dues | 5.00 |

Mr. Young's wife and two children, for whom he is legally responsible, are currently receiving public assistance.

*Case Situation No. 2*

Mr. Donald Wilson resides with six dependents in a seven-room unfurnished apartment. Mr. Wilson is employed as an automobile salesman and his gross wages are $4000.00 per week. He is employed five days a week and spends $10.00 a day carfare. He spends $50.00 a work day for lunch. His weekly salary deductions are as follows:

| | |
|---|---|
| Federal Income Tax | $705.50 |
| State Income Tax | 150.00 |
| City Income Tax | 97.00 |
| Social Security | 301.00 |
| New York State Disability Insurance | 52.50 |
| Union Dues | Not Union Member |

Mr. Wilson is the only wage earner in his present household. His legal wife and minor child, for whom he is legally responsible, are both receiving public assistance.

NOTE: *When answering Questions 18 through 21, refer to Case Situation No. 1.*

18. The *weekly amount* that Mr. Young contributes toward Social Security, New York State Disability Insurance, Income Taxes, and Union Dues is, most nearly,

   A. $214.70    B. $250.50    C. $320.50    D. $370.50

18.____

19. The *total amount* of all weekly expenses incident to Mr. Young's employment which should be deducted from his weekly gross earnings, is, most nearly,

   A. $214.70    B. $250.50    C. $370.50    D. $420.50

19.____

20. *Which one* of the following amounts is Mr. Young's *semimonthly net income?*

   A. $1259.00    B. $1363.90    C. $1623.90    D. $1701.50

20.____

21. The *semi-monthly amount* of income available to the contribution to Mr. Young's wife and two children is, most nearly,

   A. $0.00    B. $23.90    C. $236.10    D. $551.10

21.____

NOTE: When answering Questions 22 through 25, refer to Case Situation No. 2.

22. The *weekly amount* that Mr. Wilson contributes toward Social Security, New York State Disability Insurance, Federal Income Tax, and Union Dues is, most nearly,

   A. $1059.00    B. $1159.00    C. $1306.00    D. $1406.00

22.____

23. The *total amount* of all weekly expenses incident to Mr. Wilson's employment, which should be deducted from his weekly gross earnings, is, most nearly,

   A. $1159.00    B. $1306.00    C. $1406.00    D. $1606.00

23.____

24. The *semi-monthly family allowance* for Mr. Wilson and his six dependents is, most nearly,

   A. $2594.00    B. $3205.00    C. $3555.00    D. $4000.00

24.____

25. The *semi-monthly amount* of Mr. Wilson's income available for contribution to his wife and child is, most nearly,

   A. $1633.00    B. $2065.40    C. $2594.00    D. $2810.20

25.____

# KEY (CORRECT ANSWERS)

| | | | |
|---|---|---|---|
| 1. | D | 11. | D |
| 2. | A | 12. | B |
| 3. | A | 13. | A |
| 4. | C | 14. | C |
| 5. | D | 15. | D |
| 6. | A | 16. | C |
| 7. | C | 17. | A |
| 8. | B | 18. | B |
| 9. | B | 19. | C |
| 10. | A | 20. | B |

| | |
|---|---|
| 21. | A |
| 22. | A |
| 23. | C |
| 24. | C |
| 25. | B |

# EXAMINATION SECTION
## TEST 1

DIRECTIONS: Each question or incomplete statement is followed by several suggested answers or completions. Select the one that BEST answers the question or completes the statement. *PRINT THE LETTER OF THE CORRECT ANSWER IN THE SPACE AT THE RIGHT.*

1. A supervisor should consider a social worker to be skilled in diagnosis if, of the following, the worker excels in

   A. categorizing behavior, personality, and social problems in syndrome classes using a standardized nomenclature
   B. relating diagnoses to a theoretical system such as Freudian, Adlerian, Rogerian, etc.
   C. describing the person, problem, and setting as related to the casework situation
   D. determining the genesis of the problems for which the client seeks help

   1.____

2. The one of the following which is the BASIC difference between the function of a supervisor and the function of a consultant in a large social agency is that the supervisor

   A. is a permanent staff member, while the consultant is a person brought in from the outside
   B. trains young and experienced workers, while the consultant trains those who no longer need supervision
   C. has administrative responsibility for agency operation, while the consultant has no direct administrative responsibility
   D. has a personal relationship with the worker, while the consultant provides administrative controls for evaluating the supervisor

   2.____

3. Experts in social work supervision have stated that the role of the supervisor should be *authoritative* rather than *authoritarian.*
   Of the following, this means MOST NEARLY that the supervisor's authority should come from

   A. his superior skill and competence
   B. his ability to exercise democratic control
   C. responsibility delegated through administrative channels
   D. differences in role perception of the worker and the supervisor

   3.____

4. Assume that a supervisor who finds himself immobilized in the face of a difficult problem complains because his subordinates are confused and indecisive.
   Of the following, it is MOST probable that the supervisor

   A. needs to give more guidance to his subordinates so that they will be able to make decisions within their sphere of responsibility
   B. is projecting his own state of mind on to his subordinates and is venting his feelings of frustration on their incompetence
   C. requires professional help for a personality problem which may make him unsuited for supervisory responsibility
   D. should arrange for his subordinates to get special training in decision-making within their areas of responsibility

   4.____

5. A supervisor in a large agency with a recent graduate of a school of social work on his staff should be aware that the one of the following which is a common problem of the new professional worker is a tendency to

    A. interpret agency rules and regulations literally because of the desire for supervisory approval

    B. feel frustrated because agency rules and regulations prevent him from making independent decisions based on his professional training

    C. make independent decisions without calling upon the supervisor for expert advice and guidance

    D. protect himself from situations of stress by working with his clients in a routine, uninspired manner

5.\_\_\_\_

6. Assume that your agency has a serious shortage of professional staff. However, an analysis of the daily tasks of professional social workers reveals that many of the tasks performed are of a clerical or administrative nature.
Of the following, the MOST appropriate step to take FIRST in order to alleviate the shortage is to

    A. hire indigenous paraprofessionals from the community to take over part of the job load

    B. assign clerical and administrative staff to take over these non-professional tasks

    C. survey professional social workers in order to determine whether some of these clerical or administrative tasks are superfluous

    D. determine how many additional professional social workers are needed and arrange for recruitment in accordance with requirements

6.\_\_\_\_

7. Experts have made a distinction between the formal and the informal organization of a large agency.
Of the following, the informal organization has been described as

    A. dysfunctional due to its inevitable conflict with the basic objectives of the agency

    B. those levels of the agency which are separate from the administrative units which have direct responsibility for policy formulation

    C. including only those positions within the agency which have no direct responsibility for its service delivery function

    D. those relationships and channels of communication that resourceful employees develop and use in order to get the work done

7.\_\_\_\_

8. The term *bureaucracy* has invidious implications for the general public. To the social scientist, however, *bureaucracy* is a technical term for a large, complex organization .
Of the following, according to the social scientist, a *bureaucracy* is structured on rational principles and characterized by

    A. a democratic system in which each person has maximum freedom to make his own decisions

    B. a strict and well-defined hierarchy of authority functioning on the basis of clear-cut chain of command principles

    C. the assignment of independent responsibility to administrative and professional personnel responsible for delivery of services

    D. equal accessibility of all personnel within program units of the agency to personnel at the level where decisions are made

8.\_\_\_\_

9. In the hierarchical administrative organization which is characteristic of a large agency,   9.____
levels of authority emanate from the top downward.
Of the following, this structure has a tendency toward

    A. decreasing opportunities for staff participation in areas beyond their immediately circumscribed responsibilities
    B. easing the communications flow between departmental lines at the lower levels of the hierarchy
    C. permitting the flow of communication from the top downward, but not from the bottom upward
    D. structural flexibility which adapts readily to changing demands upon the organization

10. Of the following, adherence to *democratic* principles in the administration of a large   10.____
agency means MOST NEARLY

    A. the feeling of all employees that they are participating in planning and policy making
    B. an equal voice for all employees in planning and policy making
    C. relevant participation of all employees according to their special competence
    D. friendliness, regardless of rank, among all employees at all levels

11. The one of the following which is the MOST important reason that all social workers who   11.____
work in large agencies should be well-oriented to the administrative process is that they will

    A. be better qualified to participate in planning, decision-making, and formulation of policies
    B. be more sensitive to the needs of extra-agency components in the agency administrative system
    C. have a greater capacity to contribute to the agency and to accept their responsibilities within the system of cooperative effort
    D. be qualified for appointment to positions which do not include direct involvement in service

12. By virtue of training and orientation, social workers are well aware of personality traits   12.____
that enhance or diminish administrative competence. Social agencies are becoming increasingly conscious, however, of the importance of understanding the effects of different forms of agency organization and structure, not only in relation to staff performance but also in relation to the service the agency performs.
Of the following, this statement means MOST NEARLY that

    A. administrative difficulties can be analyzed and resolved, not only in terms of personality shortcomings of given individuals but also in terms of organizational arrangements
    B. such factors in agency organization as size, physical arrangements, and organizational roles can be more important than personality traits of administrators in influencing effective delivery of services
    C. agency organization and structure can have a significant effect on staff performance
    D. social workers should give more emphasis to the importance of understanding the effects of agency organization and structure, rather than personality traits

13. According to the task-centered concept of administrative organization, attention is focused on the problem or task at hand, involving all persons who may have a contribution to make, regardless of their professional status or rank in the organization.
Of the following, the MOST probable result of such an approach to agency administration would be to

    A. increase delegation of responsibility from the top downward
    B. increase promotion opportunities for non-professionals
    C. enhance the opportunities for staff to participate in policy formulations
    D. interfere with hierarchical distribution of authority from the top downward

13.____

14. The one of the following which CORRECTLY describes the change of focus in social work today is:

    A. New psychological studies and research on human behavior have resulted in increased emphasis on personality problems and the need to change individual dependency patterns
    B. The psychoanalytic orientation and the emphasis on personality problems are being challenged by social science perspectives which stress the environmental causes of individual maladjustment
    C. Emphasis on giving clients supportive assistance with personal problems and on changing individual behavior patterns has shifted to heightened attention to decreasing dependency through required work programs
    D. Sociological studies and other research in the social sciences have resulted in a new emphasis on changing family life and substituting communal ways of living for obsolete institutions

14.____

15. The one of the following which is an important distinction between the profession of social work and many other professions is that

    A. there is a basic conflict between social workers' professional interests and the interests of the agency in which they are employed
    B. there is little activity by social workers in the direction of private practice
    C. the claim for recognition of social work as a profession arose when it was practiced mainly within administrative organizations
    D. social workers have a tendency to move from private practice to practice within administrative organizations

15.____

16. As the supervisor for the After Hours Emergency Child Care Services, you have been asked by a group of home aides whether they could go out in pairs to areas of the city where they feel uneasy and where some of them have had unpleasant experiences. They point out that caseworkers have approval for this although they usually visit these neighborhoods during daytime hours, while home aides are in the field at all hours of the night. Of the following, your BEST response would be to

    A. remind the home aides that they knew the working conditions when they were hired
    B. question the statement that caseworkers have approval to go in the field in pairs
    C. sympathize with the home aides' fears and agree that their work presents many challenges
    D. indicate that you will consider each such request on an individual basis so that all possible protective measures can be taken

16.____

17. At a meeting of your supervisory staff, several supervisors inform you that they lack staff    17.____
to provide coverage for all service requests. Some units are more overburdened than
others because some kinds of service requests are more numerous. A group of caseworkers have suggested to their supervisors that all service requests be distributed
throughout the units, instead of continuing the present system of sending requests to
specialized units.
Of the following, your BEST immediate response to this proposal would be to

    A. indicate that assignment of work is not a decision to be made by casework staff,
but that you will forward the suggestion to your supervisor
    B. point out that, although you have made this serious situation known at higher lev-
els, you do not have the authority to reorganize your units in the manner suggested
    C. ask the supervisors to submit more factual data on volume, distribution of cases,
and staff available, along with their recommendations as to the feasibility of the
caseworkers' proposal
    D. draft a memo to your supervisor stating that staff shortages are now so serious
that caseworkers cannot cover all service requests, and ask for instructions

18. An institution or group home is usually the BEST placement for    18.____

    A. children who are committed by the court because of neglect or abuse by their par-
ents
    B. adolescents and school-age children who have temporarily lost their ability to
relate to parent substitutes
    C. pre-school age children whose parents cannot care for them temporarily
    D. children who have difficulty relating to their peers

19. Foster homes must be periodically re-examined as a requirement for continued licensing.    19.____
Of the following, the MOST important reason for this requirement is that

    A. homes that have been used for many years tend to deteriorate and may need to be
closed
    B. child welfare workers often do not see the foster fathers at any other time
    C. foster parents may become overwhelmed by too many placements and may desire
to have their homes closed
    D. changes in the composition and competence of a foster family should be evaluated
and reported regularly

20. A child welfare agency can USUALLY expect that new foster parents who have children    20.____
of their own will

    A. take on the role of foster parents with very little difficulty
    B. need more help than childless couples in adjusting to their new roles
    C. need to have their responsibilities to their foster children clearly differentiated from
their responsibilities to their own children
    D. have a good understanding of the needs of foster children and adjust quickly to the
agency's role in providing care for them

21. When a young child makes repeated attempts to break through the reasonable limits    21.____
which his foster parents have set on his behavior, it is PROBABLY a sign that

    A. the foster parents are not punishing him appropriately for his misbehavior
    B. he does not respect parental authority

C. he is testing whether his foster parents care enough about him to discipline him
D. the foster parents should be more lenient with him

22. Adoptive parents should be provided with factual information about the child's natural parents MAINLY

    A. in order to be able to answer his questions about his natural parents
    B. because they would try to obtain this information anyway
    C. so that they can be prevented from worrying about the child's background
    D. to encourage them to tell the child about his natural parents

22.____

23. Foster parents are usually responsible for transporting and accompanying their foster children to various appointments arranged by the child welfare worker.
When a foster parent informs the worker that he is unable to keep a specific appointment, the worker should

    A. accompany the child to the appointment himself
    B. insist that the foster parent keep the appointment
    C. reschedule the appointment for a time more convenient for the foster parent
    D. evaluate whether cancellation of the appointment would be harmful, and act accordingly

23.____

24. After spending several months in a congregate shelter, John is to be placed in a foster home with his younger siblings. However, the discharge physical reveals that he needs a tonsillectomy.
In this situation, the child welfare worker should FIRST

    A. ask the shelter to arrange for John's tonsillectomy and postpone the placement until after the operation
    B. ask the doctor if he considers the tonsillectomy to be urgent so the worker can decide whether or not to postpone the placement
    C. arrange for the tonsillectomy at once and have John hospitalized
    D. tell the prospective foster mother about the need for the tonsillectomy so she can decide when the surgery should be done

24.____

25. An eight-month-old baby, born with withdrawal symptoms and abandoned by her drug-addicted mother, is being made ready for placement in a foster home.
In this situation, the child welfare worker should

    A. not tell the prospective foster parents about the natural mother's drug addiction so that they won't become unduly worried
    B. tell the prospective foster parents about the natural mother's addiction but assure them that the child has been treated and cured
    C. inform the prospective foster parents of the child's background, explain that she may have a convulsion, and tell them what to do if this should happen
    D. not tell the prospective foster parents about the child's background unless they ask

25.____

# KEY (CORRECT ANSWERS)

| | | | |
|---|---|---|---|
| 1. | C | 11. | C |
| 2. | C | 12. | A |
| 3. | A | 13. | C |
| 4. | B | 14. | B |
| 5. | B | 15. | C |
| 6. | B | 16. | D |
| 7. | D | 17. | C |
| 8. | B | 18. | B |
| 9. | A | 19. | D |
| 10. | C | 20. | C |

| | |
|---|---|
| 21. | C |
| 22. | A |
| 23. | D |
| 24. | B |
| 25. | C |

# TEST 2

DIRECTIONS:   Each question or incomplete statement is followed by several suggested answers or completions. Select the one that BEST answers the question or completes the statement. *PRINT THE LETTER OF THE CORRECT ANSWER IN THE SPACE AT THE RIGHT.*

1.  Of the following, the BEST placement for a twelve-year-old boy who has been diagnosed       1.____
    as having a severe behavior disorder would probably be in a(n)

    A.   small group home which is programmed to offer a permissive living atmosphere
         and home instruction from the State Department of Education
    B.   institution geared to treat pre-delinquent children
    C.   foster home where his acting out behavior would be understood and accepted
    D.   institution where his behavior would be controlled through routines, discipline, and
         relationships with adults and peers

2.  In planning services for a young woman expecting an out-of-wedlock child, the child wel-       2.____
    fare worker should be PRIMARILY concerned with

    A.   obtaining as much information as possible about the young woman's ethnic back-
         ground and health history
    B.   determining how the young woman's family is reacting to the situation and whether
         they will help plan for the unborn child
    C.   making up a list of suitable adoption agencies to which the young woman can be
         referred
    D.   providing the young woman with information about all the various arrangements
         she can make for her unborn child

3.  A foster mother who has been caring for two retarded preschool children, and receiving a       3.____
    special board rate for the foster care, has become very tired. Her doctor has told her that
    she needs a vacation, and she so informs the child welfare worker. However, she does
    not wish to give up caring for the children.
    Of the following, the BEST approach for the worker to take is to

    A.   recognize the foster mother's need for a vacation and make temporary arrange-
         ments for the care of the children
    B.   remind the foster mother that she is receiving a special board rate which should be
         enough to provide her with babysitting relief
    C.   find a new facility for the children since the foster mother's health is apparently fail-
         ing as a result of taking care of the children
    D.   try to determine if there is another reason for the foster mother's exhaustion

4.  In planning for 18-month-old twins, one who appears to be developing normally and one       4.____
    who is functioning below normal and has many physical problems, the child welfare
    worker should place the GREATEST emphasis on

    A.   placing them in one foster home since research has shown that a symbiotic rela-
         tionship exists between twins
    B.   placing them separately since it would be psychologically harmful for the *normal*
         twin to live with his *abnormal* sibling

C. finding an institution that has a specially trained staff for taking care of handi-capped children but also accepts *normal* children so that the twins could remain together
D. finding an appropriate placement for each child according to his needs, realizing that meeting their individual needs is more important than their twin-ship

5. A mother has had all five of her children in placement since she was hospitalized for mental illness three years ago. The hospital has now discharged her, and she is receiv-ing follow-up treatment in an after-care clinic where she receives her medication. She wants her children back, and the clinic approves. The private agency, however, feels that the mother is not ready and also reports that the children do not want to go home. Of the following, the BEST course of action for you, as a supervisor, to take is to

    5.____

A. recommend that the children be returned to their mother as soon as possible since the clinic approves
B. keep the children in placement until the private agency feels that the mother is ready to cope with them and that they want to go back to her
C. refer the case to your psychiatric consultant and be guided by his recommendation
D. confer with representatives of the private agency and the clinic to determine if and when the children should be returned, and how to prepare the mother and children for eventual reunion

6. A child welfare worker in one of your units reports that a mother with whom she is work-ing claims that the school is discriminating against her children because she is a welfare recipient. Her children have a history of truancy and poor school achievement. The child welfare worker feels that the mother's assessment of the situation has some validity. Of the following, the BEST course of action for you to suggest to your worker is to

    6.____

A. support the mother's defense of her children and report the alleged discrimination on the part of the school to the Board of Education
B. inquire further into the reasons for the children's truancy and poor achievement with the children, the mother, and school officials
C. explore with the mother her feelings about receiving public assistance and encour-age her to find a job so she won't need assistance
D. disengage herself from her close involvement in this case since she has stopped being objective

7. It is standard practice, in providing service to children in their own homes, for the child welfare worker to work directly with the child when

    7.____

A. it is determined that his parents have no emotional problem
B. his problems are primarily in the school and community
C. he needs help in coping with his living situation and in accepting parental limita-tions
D. his parents do not speak English and the worker needs an interpreter

8. Which one of the following statements regarding the provision of services to children in their own homes is CORRECT?

    8.____

A. The caretaking parent is the primary client.
B. Services for the child under six are generally provided through the parents.
C. The way the home is kept is of primary importance in evaluating the case.
D. The most pertinent service is the one given directly to the child.

9. Of the following, the MOST important problem in the development of group day care ser-    9.____
vices for infants is that this service

   A. requires many safeguards to protect the child's physical health and emotional
      development
   B. costs too much for the parents or the community to support
   C. cannot be licensed by the Board of Health or State Department of Social Services
   D. is looked upon by the community with disfavor because people, in general, feel that
      mothers should stay home with infants

10. A child welfare worker should offer day care services    10.____

   A. to every mother on her caseload
   B. to mothers on her caseload who have the necessary motivation and strength to
      work but must provide for the care of their children during the day
   C. only to those mothers on her caseload who are already working and could take
      their children out of placement if day care services were available
   D. only to parents who have several children and are receiving supplementary assis-

11. The one of the following which is an important, although not the primary, function of a    11.____
homemaker, from the point of view of the child welfare agency, is to

      tance which could be cut off if the mother went to work
   A. interpret foster care services to the family
   B. provide the family with counseling services, as needed, in relation to the problems
      the homemaker encounters in her work with the family
   C. provide the child welfare worker with additional information about the family which
      might not be obtained otherwise, and which could be used in further planning with
      the family
   D. help the mother to understand her feelings of inadequacy as a parent and to face
      reality

12. A mother who is legally married to someone not the father of her illegitimate child wants    12.____
to surrender the child legally for adoption. Her husband does not know about the child.
The child welfare worker should advise her that she may have difficulty in legally sur-
rendering the child unless she

   A. signs a surrender and swears her husband is not the child's father
   B. informs her husband about the child and can obtain his written denial of paternity
   C. tells the court the child's real father abandoned her and the child
   D. can prove that she and her husband cannot care for the child properly

13. In planning for the placement of a ten-year-old child in foster care, it is standard practice    13.____
for the child welfare worker to

   A. make the decision with the parents, without including the child in the planning
   B. enlist the child's participation to the fullest extent possible, depending on his level
      of maturity
   C. have the parents take responsibility for preparing the child for placement
   D. help the child to accept the agency's and his parents' decision since he cannot do
      anything about it

14. Of the following, the MOST important reason that child welfare agencies should place more emphasis upon early case finding is in order to

    A. help more families obtain needed public assistance
    B. offer families more extensive diagnostic evaluation
    C. prevent separation of children from their parents
    D. provide more extensive referral services

14.____

15. If a parent accused of child neglect refuses protective service, the caseworker should inform him that

    A. he does not have the right to refuse protective service since this service is manda-tory
    B. the child will be removed from the home as soon as a foster home can be found
    C. the problem may be referred to the jurisdiction of the Family Court as the result of his refusal
    D. any further complaints of child neglect against him will be investigated by the agency and reported to the police if substantiated

15.____

16. As a supervisor, you are asked to work on a committee which is planning for the appro-priate use of case aides in family and child welfare programs.
Of the following, the one which would be the LEAST appropriate assignment for a case aide is

    A. determining, as a result of interviewing the client, the best solution to his family problems
    B. helping a parent to attend an important school meeting by caring for his children at home during the meeting
    C. finding and suggesting recipes to make a client's medically required diet more appetizing and palatable
    D. visiting an overburdened parent's home in order to suggest how to divide some of the home chores among the children

16.____

17. As a Supervisor II, you observe that the two case aides assigned to your area, who attend school parttime, are not given many work assignments. You discuss this situation with the Supervisors I, who state that it is too time-consuming to design appropriate tasks for the case aides since they are not available for a full day's work. The Supervisors I express their willingness to have the case aides do their school assignments in the office.
Of the following, your BEST response would be that the

    A. Supervisors I should see to it that the case aides do not do homework in the office because it would give the clients a bad impression
    B. Supervisors I must assign appropriate tasks to case aides so that the agency and its clients may derive the maximum benefit from their time on the job
    C. agency has great confidence in the use of parapro-fessionals
    D. schools are able to adjust their schedules for case aides and that Supervisors I should be able to do the same

17.____

18. As a supervisor, you are asked to help obtain assistance for a group of residents of your geographic area who have taken a number of unrelated children into their homes and are caring for them at their own expense.
Of the following, the MOST accurate information you can give this group is:

    A. There is no legal basis for meeting their requests
    B. Home Relief is not available as a means of providing for some of the cost of a child's care in a non-related home
    C. An ADC grant can be made for child care to friends of the child's parents who are now supporting the child
    D. They can apply to the Bureau of Child Welfare for certification as foster parents for these children and for payment of foster home boarding care rates

18.____

19. Mr. and Mrs. A are requesting the discharge from foster care of Mary, their eight-year-old daughter, who was placed voluntarily six weeks ago after the child told her teacher that Mr. A *bothered* her. Although Mary had given an elaborate account of this alleged sexual molestation, both parents denied that such an incident occurred, but requested placement as a way of relieving the tension in the home.
As the supervisor asked to participate in the decision about the parent's request for Mary's discharge from placement, your MAIN consideration should be

    A. the dynamics involved in differentiating between a child's fantasy and reality
    B. Mary's feelings about returning home to her family
    C. the factors that went into the earlier decision for placement
    D. that cases of alleged sexual molestation can be handled by court action only

19.____

20. As a supervisor on call for consultation on decisions to be made by the emergency night child welfare staff, you are asked to approve by telephone the discharge of a seven-year-old boy to his father. The boy had been admitted to a city children's shelter when his mother, who was separated from his father, died suddenly during surgery.
Of the following pieces of information supplied by the child welfare worker over the phone, which is the LEAST relevant to your decision? The

    A. father and child know each other
    B. child is in reasonably good health
    C. father has arranged with his mother to look after his son while he is at work
    D. father does not know whether the mother had initiated divorce proceedings

20.____

21. As a supervisor in the foster home program, you receive a request for a change of case worker from a foster mother who is caring for four adolescents. The mother complains that the case worker spends too much time with the children when he visits. In a conference with you, the Supervisor I, who had worked with this foster home until his recent promotion, states his belief that his positive relationship with the foster mother is more important than her relationship with the present case worker. He, therefore, wants to keep the foster home within his unit but assign it to a different case worker. He is concerned that any other course of action might result in the foster mother's request for removal of the children from her home.
Your conference with the Supervisor I on this situation should focus on the

    A. difficulty involved in securing homes for four adolescents
    B. rights of foster parents to request removal of foster children

21.____

C. rights of foster parents to request a different case worker
D. way in which the Supervisor I sees his enabling role

22. As the supervisor for the After Hours Emergency Child Care Services, you recognize, while reviewing the reports of the previous night's activities, the name of a five-year-old boy who had been reported as a runaway two weeks earlier. The current report again indicates that the police found the child wandering in the street at 3:00 A.M. about six blocks from his grandmother's house, where he has been living for the past six months. The current report also indicates that the grandmother arrived at the police station and took the boy home before any action was taken by the Emergency Child Care staff. Of the following, the LEAST valid focus for your next group conference with your staff in discussing this case would be to

    22.____

    A. stress the advisability of placement of children referred for the second time in a two-week period
    B. discuss critical indices of potential difficulties that may be present when a five-year-old child is a chronic runaway
    C. review indices for referring emergency situations that are overtly resolved after hours to the regular unit the next day
    D. develop a workshop on how to interview children

23. As a Supervisor II in a Protective Services section, you are reviewing a case record forwarded to you by the Supervisor I of one of your units, to show you how promptly his case workers have been making field visits on new referrals. In this case, the case worker visited the home within an hour after receipt of an anonymous report of neglect of an infant. The record stated that the worker was impressed by the mother's politeness and the cleanliness of the home, that the allegation of neglect was false, and that no follow-up was indicated.
Of the following, your MAIN emphasis in reviewing this case material should be on

    23.____

    A. determining how the case worker interpreted to the mother the reason for his visit
    B. finding out whether the baby was seen during the case worker's visit to the home
    C. planning to compliment the Supervisor I on having helped his caseworkers to make field visits promptly
    D. determining whether or not the record shows that the anonymous complaint was actually disproved

24. As a Supervisor II in an adoption program, you notice that the Supervisor I of one of your units presents about four times as many atypical situations for your review and approval as the Supervisor I of any other unit under your supervision.
Of the following, the BEST step for you take FIRST in order to evaluate the significance of this observation would be to

    24.____

    A. recognize that, because many children are hard to place, no family that offers to adopt a child should be eliminated
    B. accept the fact that all atypical situations should be reviewed carefully because adoption policies are changing rapidly
    C. analyze the handling of all the studies initiated within this unit during a specific time span in order to determine if appropriate action has been taken in every case
    D. become aware that the supervisors of the other units are probably rejecting atypical situations without bringing them to your attention

25. As a supervisor, you read at night a newspaper report on a serious fire in an apartment     25.____
building in your work area in which a number of children suffered from severe burns and
smoke inhalation, and were admitted to X Hospital. The next morning, the MOST appropriate action for the district office to take would be to

   A. explore whether or not X Hospital sees evidence of abuse or neglect of any of the
      children hospitalized and, if so, whether the hospital plans to refer the children and
      families to the Bureau of Child Welfare
   B. initiate steps for referral for re-housing
   C. send a worker to the area to determine how or if he can be of help
   D. send a worker to the hospital to offer family and child welfare services

————

# KEY (CORRECT ANSWERS)

|     |   |     |   |
|-----|---|-----|---|
| 1.  | D | 11. | C |
| 2.  | D | 12. | B |
| 3.  | A | 13. | B |
| 4.  | D | 14. | C |
| 5.  | D | 15. | C |
| 6.  | B | 16. | A |
| 7.  | C | 17. | B |
| 8.  | B | 18. | D |
| 9.  | A | 19. | C |
| 10. | B | 20. | D |

|     |   |
|-----|---|
| 21. | D |
| 22. | A |
| 23. | D |
| 24. | C |
| 25. | A |

————

# TEST 3

DIRECTIONS: Each question or incomplete statement is followed by several suggested answers or completions. Select the one that BEST answers the question or completes the statement. *PRINT THE LETTER OF THE CORRECT ANSWER IN THE SPACE AT THE RIGHT.*

1. Of the following, the MOST important influence on the personality development of a child during the first year is the    1.____

    A. family as a whole
    B. mother
    C. way his siblings react to him
    D. relationship between the parents

2. Of the following, the terms which is GENERALLY applied to the situation in which an infant in foster care has insufficient interaction with a substitute mother is    2.____

    A. maternal rejection                    B. mothering complex
    C. maternal deprivation                  D. interaction deficiency

3. When a foster child exhibits nonconforming behavior, it is MOST important for the foster parents to be able to    3.____

    A. ignore this behavior since this is the child's way of expressing his emotional needs
    B. accept and condone this behavior as an expression of the child's insecurity
    C. use punishment and reward to force the child to conform
    D. accept this behavior without condoning it, while trying to meet the child's emotional needs

4. Separation of the infant from his mother can be a traumatic experience. The amount of emotional damage to the infant and the consequent effects on his personality depend MAINLY on the    4.____

    A. quality and consistency of the substitute mothering he receives
    B. reasons for and duration of the separation
    C. kind of preparation for separation the infant receives
    D. degree of the mother's acceptance of the placement

5. Research studies of language development in young children have shown that    5.____

    A. the multiple mothering of children in a large family retards language development
    B. language retardation in otherwise normal children is usually related to inadequate language stimulation
    C. language retardation is always associated with slow motor development
    D. children are usually slow in learning to talk when more than one language is spoken in the home

6. The two MOST important influences on the cultural development of a seven-year-old child are the    6.____

    A. home and peer group                   B. school and peer group
    C. home and school                       D. home and church

7. In our culture, a child gains his sense of identity MAINLY from                    7.____

    A. knowledge about and experience with his parents and extended family
    B. association with members of his own ethnic group
    C. a study of the historical and ethnic factors in this culture
    D. association with his peers

8. A child who has grown up in foster care may want to talk about his natural parents,    8.____
although he has never known them.
Of the following, the BEST way for a child welfare worker to deal with this situation is to

    A. help the child to forget that he is a foster child and to relate to his foster parents as though they were his natural parents
    B. encourage the child to express his feelings and fantasies about his natural parents so that the worker can help his understand these feelings and fantasies
    C. set up a psychiatric interview for the child to determine if he is making a satisfactory adjustment to his foster child status
    D. tell the child that he can look for his natural parents when he is older

9. Of the following, the MOST important reason that those responsible for the care of a child    9.____
in placement should never depreciate the child's natural parents or the home from which
he came is that the

    A. child's self-esteem depends on how he feels about his natural parents and his previous experiences
    B. natural parents may have been incapable of being adequate parents
    C. child may feel that the substitute parents are jealous of his natural parents
    D. child will be forced into the position of defending his natural parents and will resent the substitute parents

10. The Children's Apperception Test (CAT) is a commonly used protective test for pre-    10.____
school children in which the child

    A. has an opportunity to express his fantasies and moods through drawing and painting
    B. tells a story about pictures that are shown to him
    C. completes an unfinished story
    D. is given a variety of toys and is placed in a make-believe play situation

11. Sickle cell anemia is a blood disease MOST commonly found in children whose parents    11.____
are

    A. Caucasian               B. interracial
    C. Black or Latin American     D. Oriental

12. Schizophrenia in children USUALLY becomes manifest    12.____

    A. during the latency period
    B. during adolescence only
    C. when the mother has a history of schizophrenia
    D. during early childhood or adolescence

13. Although day care was originally established mainly as a social service for working mothers, it has been found that

    A. day care can also be an educational experience for a child and help in the development of peer relationships
    B. most working mothers would prefer to leave their children with friends or relatives rather than at a day care center
    C. it would be economically feasible to make day care centers available to all mothers in the community
    D. working mothers of physically and mentally handicapped children do not benefit from day care facilities

13._____

14. In deciding on which day care center to recommend to a working mother, the MOST important of the following considerations is the

    A. educational background of the staff
    B. ratio of staff to children
    C. director of the center
    D. physical plant and recreational facilities

14._____

15. During the past few years, dramatic and serious incidents of child abuse have resulted in

    A. the passage of legislation in all states requiring medical and other designated personnel to report incidents of abuse
    B. the proliferation of child care agencies dealing with child abuse cases only
    C. a tightening of restrictions in most states on eligibility for public assistance of parents who abuse their children
    D. a slight decline in the number of child neglect cases reported to authorities and a slight increase in the number of child abuse cases reported

15._____

16. Of the following alternatives, the one which is LEAST available to the Black unwed mother in planning for her child is

    A. adoption
    B. temporary care in a small group home
    C. foster family care
    D. dependence upon her family

16._____

Questions 17-19.

DIRECTIONS: Questions 17 through 19 are to be answered by matching each of the persons listed in Column I with the field in which the person is an authority, as stated in Column II.

COLUMN I                 COLUMN II

17. Lauretta Bender           A. Group work      17._____
                            B. Homefinding
                            C. Day care

18. Fritz Redl                D. Acting out, emotionally disturbed children and adolescents      18._____

19. Gisela Konopka          E. Childhood schizophrenia      19._____

20. As a supervisor in the Division of Interagency Relationships, you become aware that a
particular voluntary child-caring agency often reports discharges of children from foster
care either on the date the discharge plan is to be implemented or shortly after the discharge has taken place. Your staff informs you that such late discharge reports are forwarded most frequently when the discharge plans indicate a need for intensive
supportive help. The BEST approach for you to take would be to meet with

    20.\_\_\_\_

    A.  your team and tell them to disapprove all such discharges in the future
    B.  your team and tell them to take all appropriate clerical action as quickly as possible
    C.  your immediate supervisor to inform him that a particular agency is making
        unsound discharges
    D.  representatives of the voluntary child-caring agency to discuss the subject of dis-
        charge practice

21. As a supervisor, you are representing the Bureau of Child Welfare on a committee that
meets bi-monthly to plan for the needs of retarded children. You note that the comments
of the parents of retardates are warmly accepted at each session, but are never incorpo-
rated into the minutes or included in recommendations for follow-up action.
Of the following, the BEST approach for you to take would be to

    21.\_\_\_\_

    A.  report this discrepancy to your immediate supervisor
    B.  attempt to maneuver the group so that the parents of retardates will be encouraged
        to make more comments at committee meetings
    C.  raise a question at the next regular meeting about the discrepancy you have found
        in the recording of participation by parents
    D.  talk to several parents after the next meeting to find out if they object to the manner
        in which minutes are recorded

22. As a Supervisor II, you note that your staff appears to make minimal use of community
resources to meet client needs. When you discuss this at a staff meeting, you meet a
great deal of resistance from both the Supervisors I and the case workers, who say: *You
are not out there.*
Of the following, your BEST response in this situation would be to

    22.\_\_\_\_

    A.  refer to an article you have read about how workers can involve themselves in the
        community
    B.  ask for volunteers for a committee to explore possible resources in the community
        they serve
    C.  ask the group to give examples of their use of community resources
    D.  ask the group to describe their experiences in seeking out community resources

23. As a supervisor, you are invited as an expert consultant to meet with a community group
discussing child day care needs. At the meeting, one parent urges the establishment of
group care for infants in her apartment building, where there are about ten infants
between the ages of three and twelve months.
Of the following, the FIRST suggestion you should make concerning this proposal is
that

    23.\_\_\_\_

    A.  those parents in the building who are interested in infant care attend a meeting to
        discuss the specific needs of his own infant and what his expectations of group
        care are

B. the group invite an expert on infant development to its next meeting for the purpose of outlining a possible infant group care program

C. the community group insure that pediatric consultation would be available to the persons providing the infant group care

D. one parent contact the landlord of the apartment building to inquire about regulations or stipulations for use of an apartment or other building facility for an infant group care program

24. Of the following, the MOST desirable pattern to utilize in community planning of child welfare services is to

A. leave each agency in the community free to develop those services which its constituency feels strongly about and wishes to support

B. have each agency in the community assigned a particular function by the state licensing authority in line with community need

C. consult a central planning body, representative of all agencies in the community, when any agency is considering developing a new service or dropping an old one

D. merge all agencies in the community providing like services, in order to reduce administrative expenses

24.____

25. It is recognized that very young children should not remain in hospitals after the condition for which they were admitted is under control and can be managed outside the hospital setting.
Of the following, the BEST method for preventing well children from remaining in hospitals longer than necessary is for

A. hospital policy to provide for referral of children to the Bureau of Child Welfare when the hospital staff believe parents may not be able to take their children home as soon as they are medically well

B. hospital social service departments to prepare social histories on children hospitalized, focusing especially on children *at risk*

C. the public child welfare agency to receive on a regular basis lists of children remaining in hospitals

D. hospitals to send to child caring agencies lists of children not discharged, although medically well

25.____

# KEY (CORRECT ANSWERS)

| | | | | |
|---|---|---|---|---|
| 1. | B | | 11. | C |
| 2. | C | | 12. | D |
| 3. | D | | 13. | A |
| 4. | A | | 14. | B |
| 5. | B | | 15. | A |
| | | | | |
| 6. | C | | 16. | A |
| 7. | A | | 17. | E |
| 8. | B | | 18. | D |
| 9. | A | | 19. | A |
| 10. | B | | 20. | D |

| | |
|---|---|
| 21. | C |
| 22. | D |
| 23. | A |
| 24. | C |
| 25. | A |

———————

# EXAMINATION SECTION
# TEST 1

**Directions:** Each question or incomplete statement is followed by several suggested answers or completions. Select the one the BEST answers the question or completes the statement. *PRINT THE LETTER OF THE CORRECT ANSWER IN THE SPACE AT THE RIGHT.*

1)    The primary sources of data in most assessments are                1. _____

A.    completed assessment forms
B.    the client's verbal statements
C.    psychological test results
D.    collateral sources

2)    A social worker is fulfilling the role of a "mediator" when he or she    2. _____

A.    calls attention to the probable social consequences to a new housing development
B.    refers a jobless person to an unemployment agency
C.    evaluates the outcome of a colleague's practice
D.    helps a frustrated wife to clarify her position to a husband

3)    In the systems model of human behavior, "division of labor" is an    3. _____
example of

A.    autopoiesis
B.    social control
C.    differentiation
D.    hierarchy

4)    After several weeks of behavioral intervention, a child is consistently    4. _____
performing the desired behavior targeted by his parents and a social worker: that
is, he is going to bed at the correct time without argument or delaying tactics.
Now that he's reached this stage, the social worker recommends that the parents
gradually withdraw the prompts and reinforcements that induced the behavior to begin
with. This is an example of

A.    extinction
B.    shaping
C.    fading
D.    modeling

5)    When working with a group, a social worker encourages decision-making    5. _____
by consensus. Drawbacks to the use of consensus include

A.    involvement of few available group resources
B.    alienation of the minority
C.    time- and energy-intensiveness
D.    decreased likelihood of handling future controversies

6) The primary rationale for the use of a social history for client assessment is that          6. _____

A. past behavior is the best predictor of future behavior
B. the best source of information about a client's situation is the client her/himself
C. the best protection against legal liability is an exhaustive data set
D. problems exist because of an unbalanced reaction between a client system and the environment

7) Most professional codes of ethics provide that a social worker's primary ethical duty is to          7. _____

A. respect client privacy and confidentiality
B. challenge social injustice
C. work in the best interest of clients
D. avoid situations that involve ethical conflicts

8) In agency planning, which of the following visual aids will be MOST useful in helping to examine the benefits and drawbacks of different alternative choices?          8. _____

A. Task planning sheet
B. Gantt chart
C. Decision tree
D. PERT chart

9) Which of the following questions or statements is MOST appropriate for a practitioner in initiating an interview?          9. _____

A. "I understand you have a problem."
B. "You came in here to see me about _____."
C. "How can I help you today?"
D. "I'm glad you came in to see me."

10) What is the term commonly used to describe children who suffer physical, mental, or emotional injuries inflicted by caretaking adults?          10. _____

A. Developmentally disabled
B. Victims
C. At risk
D. Abused or neglected

11) Typically, the questioning process in a social work interview should progress          11. _____

A. chronologically
B. from general to specific
C. from specific to general
D. in a series of grouped topical units

12) Assessment is a process that is considered to be the task of the          12. _____

A. agency psychiatrist or clinician
B. social worker
C. client
D. social worker and client together

13) A social worker who wants to use a small group as a resource for clients          13. _____
should remember the general rule that the addition of new members, especially
resistant ones, should be avoided during the _____ stage of group
development.

A. differentiation
B. intimacy
C. preaffiliation
D. power and control

14) During an assessment interview with a male high school student, it          14. _____
becomes clear to the practitioner that the boy's behavior problems are related
in some way to his frustration at the different expectations of his teachers and
his peers concerning the role of a student. The boy is experiencing

A. inter-role conflict
B. role ambiguity
C. intra-role conflict
D. role incapacity

15) When considering the use of informal resources for an intervention,          15. _____
the social worker should

A. view informal resources as an inexpensive alternative to formal services
B. whenever possible, try to "professionalize" or train informal resources to
lend them authority
C. already have some knowledge of available self-help groups in the community
D. whenever informal resources are identified, try to steer clients toward the ones
that are probably most useful

16) Probably the biggest difference between the supervisory role in social work 16. _____
and that of other professions is the

A. amount of psychological support that must be provided to supervisees
B. degree of direct involvement in the work of supervisees
C. predominant use of "soft" criteria in performance evaluations
D. greater difficulty in matching workers to tasks

17) A social worker is interviewing a woman in a mental hospital who appears   17. _____
lucid but is suspected of having some mental illness. When gathering information,
the worker should

A. explain fully the reason for the interview and ask the client to give her
opinion of her mental status
B. ask short, closed-ended assessment questions up front
C. administer a standardized assessment that may be evaluated by a psychologist
D. work assessment questions into the ordinary flow of the conversation

18)    A social worker becomes aware of a colleague's incompetent or          18. _____
unethical practice.  According to the NASW code, the worker's FIRST obligation is to

A.    inform all of the colleague's relevant clients of the situation
B.    approach the colleague to discuss his/her incapacitation, incompetence, etc.
C.    file a complaint with the NASW
D.    file a complaint with the appropriate licensing board

19)    A "communication loop" is completed when                              19. _____

A.    the person to whom the message is addressed begins to respond
B.    the person who initiates the message has completed the transmission
C.    the person to whom the message is addressed receives the message
D.    the person to whom the message is addressed decodes the message

20)    Because many parents believe in and utilize corporal punishment as    20. _____
discipline, a social worker must be able to differentiate physical abuse from
ordinary spanking or corporal punishment.  Which of the following is NOT a
useful means of making this distinction?

A.    Parent striking the child in places that are easily injured
B.    Repeated episodes of corporal punishment
C.    Child's report that punishments are severe and painful
D.    Injury to child's body tissue

21)    A social worker makes an initial in-home visit to a married couple who  21. _____
have willingly submitted to an intervention regarding their marital problems.  During
the interview the couple points out that they will be leaving the area in a few weeks,
because the wife has been transferred by her employer to a new location.  Probably
the MOST appropriate plan for dealing with this couple would involve the
_____ model of social work.

A.    person-centered
B.    cognitive-behavioral
C.    solution-focused
D.    task-centered

22)    The primary purpose of evaluative research in social work is to        22. _____

A.    measure a client's self-satisfaction
B.    determine whether outcomes can be attributed to an intervention
C.    express the effectiveness of interventions in material terms
D.    determine whether an outcome was achieved

23)    Each of the following should be used as a guideline in child placement  23. _____
decisions, EXCEPT

A.    efforts to protect the child should involve as little disruption as possible
B.    use of placement to compel a parent to take some action
C.    involvement of parents and child in the placement decision
D.    maintenance of child's cultural beliefs in placement

24) Which of the following is NOT a factor involved in the decoding of     24. _____
a message?

A. Relationship with interviewer
B. Social, emotional, and cognitive barriers
C. Ethics
D. Context of interview

25) A practitioner wants to make the parents of an adolescent aware of     25. _____
the behavioral manifestations of depression. Which of the following is LEAST
likely to be an indicator?

A. Sudden tearful reactions
B. Excessive pleasure-seeking
C. Decline in school achievement
D. Jokes about death or dying

26) Which of the following is LEAST likely to be an area of conflict between     26. _____
social workers and attorneys?

A. Confidentiality
B. Recording information
C. The best interests of a client
D. The definition of "client"

27) Which of the following typically occurs in the first stage of group therapy?   27. _____

A. The members are hostile toward the leader.
B. Cliques form within the group.
C. The members talk through the leader and seem to ignore one another.
D. The members interact with each other tend to ignore the leader.

28) In conducting employee evaluations, a social work supervisor should use    28. _____
_____ as available criteria.

     I. pre-established objective measures such as timeliness
     II. "soft" criteria such as attitude
     III. the supervisor's own work experience
     IV. the performance of others in similar assignments

A. I only
B. I and II
C. I and III
D. I, II, III and IV

29) Which of the following is NOT a term that is interchangeable with     29. _____
"stepfamily"?

A. Remarried family
B. Blended family
C. Reconstituted family
D. Renested family

30) A worker refers a client to a colleague who specializes and is trained in law, even though the client requested the service from the worker. Which of the following professional values or ethics is the worker implementing?    30. _____

A. Self-determination
B. Privacy
C. Competence
D. Confidentiality

31) Social work practice that is based on behavioral theory assumes that behaviors are determined by    31. _____

A. emotions
B. consequences
C. values
D. internal thought processes

32) Which of the following is NOT a symptom associated with bipolar disorder?    32. _____

A. Increase in goal-oriented activity
B. Distractibility
C. Significant weight loss
D. Decreased need for sleep

33) A "helping relationship" between the social worker and client is BEST described as    33. _____

A. the goal of any initial contact between worker and client
B. the medium offered to people in trouble through which they are presented with opportunities
C. the means by which a worker gains the client's trust to solve problems
D. a lifeline that is thrown to people in trouble in order to help them out of current problems

34) Communities often contain individuals who are categorized as "AFDC mothers" or "hard-core unemployed" or "AIDS patients," among others. This is a destructive application of the concept of    34. _____

A. service delivery
B. niche
C. differentiation
D. diversity

35) The first step in any single-system practice evaluation is to    35. _____

A. record baseline data
B. select suitable measures
C. implement the intervention
D. specify the goal

36)    A social worker plans a behavioral intervention for a developmentally         36. _____
disabled adult who does not look people in the eye when speaking with them.
Each of the following behavioral strategies may be useful to the intervention, EXCEPT

A.    overcorrection
B.    instruction
C.    prompting
D.    shaping

37)    During several in-home visits with a family, the mother repeatedly refuses   37. _____
to acknowledge that her alcoholism is having an adverse effect on others in the
household.  The MOST appropriate next step for the social worker would be to initiate

A.    a challenge
B.    behavioral rehearsal
C.    self-talk management
D.    a behavioral contract

38)    Working-class or low-income marriages are typically characterized by         38. _____

A.    marriage late in life
B.    flexible divisions of labor
C.    troubled mother-child relationships
D.    emotional distance between partners

39)    A researcher repeatedly measures the dependent variable throughout two       39. _____
baseline and two treatment phases of a study to assess whether variability in the
dependent variable is due to the influence of the independent variable. She is using
a(n) _____ design of measurement.

A.    AB
B.    ABAB
C.    multiple baseline
D.    Solomon four-group

40)    What is the typical time-frame for crisis intervention?                      40. _____

A.    One to two weeks
B.    Six to eight weeks
C.    At least eight weeks
D.    Six months or more, depending on the nature of the crisis

41)    Stigma, once it has become part of a culture, has certain predictable        41. _____
consequences.  Which of the following is NOT one of these consequences?

A.    Discrimination
B.    Absorption
C.    Altered self-concept
D.    Development of subculture

42) A social worker is engaged in a one-on-one interview with a 10-year-old  42. _____
boy, in order to investigate allegations of a father's sexual abuse. The allegations
were initially brought by the mother, now divorced from the father, and were later
corroborated by the boy. The mother and father are engaged in a custody battle for
the boy. The boy's account of events is extremely consistent over time, listing the
same major events in sequence, but his affect is flat--he relates his accounts of abuse
in an oddly detached manner. The BEST action for the social worker at this point would be to

A.    terminate the interview and begin criminal proceedings against the father
B.    terminate the interview and refer the child for an immediate psychiatric consultation
C.    ask the mother to join in the interview and see if her account matches the boy's
D.    ask the boy to go into greater detail about the related events, out of sequence, and then
repeat the request at a later time

43) When working with individuals or families of native American cultures,  43. _____
it is best to begin by

A.    gathering a social history
B.    using indirect approaches such as analogy or metaphor
C.    asking for open-ended descriptions of family roles
D.    direct questioning

44) In cases of elder abuse, the government may intervene if  44. _____

I.    the older person requests it
II.   the older person is found at a hearing to be incompetent
III.  the abuse or neglect presents an unacceptable level of danger to the older
person
IV.   the abuse is properly reported and recorded by a visiting social services
worker

A.    I only
B.    I and II
C.    I, II and III
D.    I, II, III and IV

45) Which of the following is a guideline that should be observed in  45. _____
developing an assessment questionnaire for clients?

A.    Develop several focused questionnaires rather than a single all-purpose one.
B.    The most sensitive or probing questions should appear near the middle of the
questionnaire.
C.    For complex ideas, form two-part questions.
D.    Include only open-ended questions.

46) During the assessment phase of an interview, checklists are most useful for  46. _____
identifying and selecting

A.    problems for intervention
B.    specific objectives
C.    available resources
D.    general goals

47)    Which of the following is an advantage associated with the family                47. _____
life-cycle model?

A.    It highlights the special challenges of blended families.
B.    It identifies developmental tasks for families at specific stages.
C.    It is especially applicable to families in minority groups.
D.    It applies to those who do not have children.

48)    Before making the decision to advocate on behalf of a client, it is              48. _____
important to consider several factors.  Which of the following is NOT one of these?

A.    Client's consent for advocacy.
B.    Whether advocating is the most useful process that can be applied to the situation.
C.    Whether the complaint or decision involves a legitimate grievance
D.    Client's knowledge and feeling about human services.

49)    Which of the following is an advantage associated with the use of               49. _____
genograms in client assessment?

A.    Targeting and identification of relevant social supports.
B.    Execution and interpretation require no instruction.
C.    Placement of an individual or family within a social context.
D.    A considerable shortening of the case record.

50)    Activities involved in social casework typically include                        50. _____

A.    counseling those with a terminal illness
B.    supervising juvenile probation clients
C.    providing job training
D.    preparing court reports

51)    In middle childhood, school-age children are generally concerned with           51. _____

A.    "good" behavior in order to receive approval from others
B.    behaving appropriately because they fear punishment
C.    the concordance of behaviors with an adopted moral code
D.    conforming with group standards in order to be rewarded

52)    When a social worker/client relationship is characterized by                    52. _____
ineffectiveness, the most common reason is that

A.    resources are not available to meet the client's needs
B.    the client has not sufficiently specified his or her needs
C.    an incorrect solution has been identified by the worker
D.    the worker is attempting to keep the relationship on a pleasant level

53)    A social history report includes the statement: "The subject claims to          53. _____
have completed high school."  This should be included under the heading:

A.    Family Background and Situation
B.    Intellectual functioning
C.    Impressions and Assessment
D.    Such a statement shouldn't appear at all in a social history report.

54) According to Erickson, which of the following stages of psychosocial development occurs FIRST in the human life span?    54. _____

A.   Initiative vs. guilt
B.   Trust vs. mistrust
C.   Identity vs. role confusion
D.   Autonomy vs. shame and doubt

55) The strategy of "reframing" is most useful for    55. _____

A.   desensitizing clients to past trauma
B.   classifying client/family problems according to standard diagnostic categories
C.   helping clients to model their own behavior after others'
D.   revealing a client's strengths and opportunities for helping

56) In general, it is believed that interviewers who spend less than a minimum    56
of _____ of an interview listening to the client are more active than they should be.

A.   one-fourth
B.   one-third
C.   one-half
D.   two thirds

57) In the _____ model of social work, the goal of the social    57. _____
worker is to enhance and restore the psychosocial functioning of persons, or to change noxious social conditions that impede the mutually beneficial interaction between person and their environment.

A.   structural-functional
B.   ecological
C.   medical
D.   strategic

58) In social work, "micro" practice usually focuses on    58. _____

A.   resolving the problems of individuals, families, or small groups
B.   planning, administration, evaluation, and community organizing
C.   developmental activities in the social environment
D.   facilitating communication, mediation, and negotiation

59) _____ theory may prove most productive for the social work    59. _____
practitioner in understanding families of homosexuals, because it introduces unambiguous distinctions between stigma and homosexual behaviors and feelings.

A.   Structural
B.   Object relations
C.   Strategic
D.   Labeling

60)     A client tells a practitioner that his main goal for intervention is to decide     60. _____
on a college major.  To BEST help this client, the practitioner will assume the role of

A.     enabler
B.     mediator
C.     initiator
D.     educator

61)     Which of the following is NOT a guideline for interacting with clients from     61. _____
a Latino culture?

A.     Efforts to foster independence and self-reliance may be interpreted by many
Latinos as a lack of concern for others.
B.     Efforts to deal one-on-one with an adolescent client may serve to alienate the
parents, especially the mother.
C.     A nonverbal gesture such as lowering the eyes is interpreted by many Latinos
as a sign of respect and deference to authority.
D.     In much of Latino culture, the locus of control for problems tends to be much
more external than internal.

62)     The broadest, most general type of plan used in social work     62. _____
administration is the

A.     plan for meeting objectives
B.     statement of goals
C.     statement of mission
D.     guiding policies

63)     In composing a social network grid with a client, which of the following     63. _____
steps is typically performed FIRST?

A.     Dividing acquaintances according to direction of help
B.     Dividing acquaintances according to duration of acquaintance
C.     Identifying people who can help the client in concrete ways
D.     Identifying areas of life in which people impact the client

64)     An administrator notices, in several trips through the agency grounds, that     64. _____
a handful of the organization's support staff are often engaged in socializing or other
nonproductive activities.  The groups are always small and never made up of the
same people, and nearly all members of the support staff have received satisfactory
evaluations from their supervisor.  The socializing does not occur around clients or
visiting professionals.  Over the past several years, the agency's efficiency record
has remained about the same.  The agency would probably be BEST served by the
view that

A.     rigid controls should be implemented to reduce this behavior
B.     a memorandum should be circulated citing this behavior as a poor example
C.     the behavior may help to relieve boredom and should be ignored
D.     the supervisor should add an item or two to the evaluation that will address this behavior

65)     Each of the following is a stage of the dying process described by          65. _____
Kübler-Ross, EXCEPT

A.     acknowledgement
B.     depression
C.     anger
D.     acceptance

66)     For a prison inmate, "notice of rights" means the inmate          66. _____

I.       receives advance notice of what conduct will result in discipline or
punishment
II.      receives written notice of any charges against him
III.     is entitled to organize a group meeting for political purposes

A.     I and II
B.     I and III
C.     II and III
D.     I, II and III

67)     Which of the following values is NOT generally indigenous to families          67. _____
of Asian heritage?

A.     Inconspicuousness
B.     Perfectionism
C.     Fatalism
D.     Shame as a behavioral influence

68)     Most professionals recommend that in order to accurately evaluate the          68. _____
effect of an intervention, baseline data should be collected for no fewer than
_____ data points.

A.     2
B.     3
C.     4
D.     5

69)     During an assessment interview, a social worker and a client try to clarify          69. _____
and analyze the client's sense of self.  If the worker wants to discover something
about the client's self-acceptance, which of the following questions is MOST appropriate?

A.     To what extent do you worry about illness and physical incapacity?
B.     Is what you expect to happen mostly good or mostly bad?
C.     Do you enjoy the times when you are alone?
D.     Where do your other family members live?

70)     Which of the following cognitive traits explains the mistaken belief held          70. _____
by many adolescents that they are invincible or protected from harmful
consequences of their behavior?

A.     The personal fable
B.     Object delusion
C.     Egocentrism
D.     Pseudohypocrisy

71)    An 18-year-old woman comes to see a social worker at a crisis center          71. _____
one day after being raped on a date.  In the interview with this client, the social
worker should FIRST:

A.    emphasize medical and legal procedures
B.    obtain factual information about the rape
C.    listen to the client and support her emotionally
D.    help the client establish contact with significant others

72)    During a client assessment, each of the following should be considered          72. _____
a useful question, EXCEPT

A.     Can you tell me about times when you've successfully handled a problem
like this in the past?
B.     When family members complain about your behavior, what to they say?
C.     How have you managed to cope up to this point?
D.     What do your friends and family seem to like most about you?

73)    Norms are MOST accurately described as          73. _____

A.    attitudes toward life events and processes
B.    assumptions about the world
C.    expectations of the self and others
D.    ideas about what is proper and desirable behavior

74)    Generally, when a homeless person or group is removed from a          74. _____
condemned or abandoned property under the law, the most significant legal question
to arise is whether

A.    the last owner of the property can be located for consent
B.    the property is being "rehabilitated" by the occupants
C.    the state recognizes a "right to shelter"
D.    the property has really been abandoned

75)    A social worker introduces herself to a family household in which an          75. _____
elderly man lives. The man has been reported by neighbors on several occasions
for making threats of violence to a number of adolescents in the neighborhood.
The worker recognizes that she is uninvited, and the BEST way for her to describe
the purpose of her relationship to the family would be as

A.    helping the man to modify his behavior so that no further institutional involvement will be
necessary
B.    helping the man to avoid the aggravating stimulus of contact with neighborhood teens
C.    protecting the neighborhood from the elderly man's threats
D.    arranging for the man to get counseling in order to understand and change his behavior

————

# KEY (CORRECT ANSWERS)

| | | | | |
|---|---|---|---|---|
| 1. | B | | 41. | B |
| 2. | D | | 42. | D |
| 3. | C | | 43. | B |
| 4. | C | | 44. | B |
| 5. | C | | 45. | A |
| | | | | |
| 6. | A | | 46. | D |
| 7. | C | | 47. | B |
| 8. | C | | 48. | D |
| 9. | B | | 49. | D |
| 10. | B | | 50. | A |
| | | | | |
| 11. | B | | 51. | A |
| 12. | D | | 52. | D |
| 13. | D | | 53. | D |
| 14. | C | | 54. | B |
| 15. | C | | 55. | D |
| | | | | |
| 16. | A | | 56. | D |
| 17. | D | | 57. | B |
| 18. | B | | 58. | A |
| 19. | A | | 59. | D |
| 20. | C | | 60. | A |
| | | | | |
| 21. | C | | 61. | D |
| 22. | B | | 62. | C |
| 23. | B | | 63. | D |
| 24. | C | | 64. | C |
| 25. | B | | 65. | A |
| | | | | |
| 26. | C | | 66. | A |
| 27. | C | | 67. | B |
| 28. | B | | 68. | B |
| 29. | D | | 69. | C |
| 30. | C | | 70. | A |
| | | | | |
| 31. | B | | 71. | C |
| 32. | C | | 72. | B |
| 33. | B | | 73. | D |
| 34. | B | | 74. | B |
| 35. | D | | 75. | A |
| | | | | |
| 36. | A | | | |
| 37. | A | | | |
| 38. | D | | | |
| 39. | B | | | |
| 40. | B | | | |

# TEST 2

**Directions:** Each question or incomplete statement is followed by several suggested answers or completions. Select the one that BEST answers the question or completes the statement. *PRINT THE LETTER OF THE CORRECT ANSWER IN THE SPACE AT THE RIGHT.*

1)    A 24-year-old mother of four, recently widowed, tells a practitioner: "I feel like my whole life has just fallen apart. I don't think I can take care of my family on my own. My husband always made all the decisions and earned the money to support us. I haven't slept well since he died and I've started drinking more often. My parents try to help me but it's not enough."

1. _____

The practitioner responds by saying: "So you're afraid about your ability to shoulder all the family responsibilities now." This response is an example of a(n)

A.    reflection
B.    clarification
C.    paraphrase
D.    summarization

2)    At the beginning of an intake interview, a social worker's tasks are to

2. _____

    I.      gather data and conduct an assessment
    II.     establish a positive relationship with the interviewee
    III.    obtain brief details that will indicate whether the situation for which the client wants help is among the problems for which the worker offers help
    IV.    offer help

A.    I only
B.    I and II
C.    II and III
D.    I, II, III and IV

3)    Which of the following is NOT a basic purpose of a professional code of ethics?

3. _____

A.    To provide a mechanism for professional accountability
B.    To educate professionals about sound conduct
C.    To set standards that will be understood and enforced across all cultures
D.    To serve as a tool for improving practice

4)      According to cognitive-behavioral theory, schemas represent a client's        4. _____

A.      subversive attempts to persist in faulty cognitions
B.      automatic responses
C.      different response patterns
D.      core beliefs and assumptions

                                                                                       5. _____

5)      Objective data found in a client's folder might include

A.      A neighbor's recorded statement about a previous incident
B.      Notes on an interview with his psychotherapist
C.      A work evaluation performed by a supervisor
D.      A summary of previous criminal convictions

6)      In the middle phase of a client interview, as a problem is being further        6. _____
explored, the practitioner should spend a considerable amount of time

A.      interpreting behavior
B.      confronting discrepancies
C.      restating or paraphrasing
D.      negotiating a service contract

7)      Which of the following statements is TRUE about social work assess-            7. _____
ment?

A.      It is another term for "goal setting."
B.      It identifies a problem and its potential impact.
C.      It refers to the search for alternative solutions.
D.      It relates to the evaluation of program effectiveness.

8)      An agency needs to write a proposal to a private foundation in order to        8. _____
request funding for renovations.  It will be necessary for the agency to organize a _____ group.

A.      training
B.      task-focused
C.      recreation
D.      self-help

9)      Social exchange theory is based on the idea that people                        9. _____

A.      often attempt to superimpose their own needs onto the desires of oth-
ers
B.      aim to protect themselves from punishment in relationships
C.      aim to maximize rewards and minimize costs in relationships
D.      exchange rewards with those who are most like themselves

10) Privileged communication typically applies in cases of                    10. _____

    I.      marital infidelity, if both spouses are participating in treatment
    II.    legal proceedings in which a practitioner is asked to produce
           client records in court
    III.   child abuse or neglect
    IV.   client disclosures of personal and sensitive information

A.    I and III
B.    I, II and IV
C.    III and IV
D.    I, II, III and IV

11) During an assessment interview, a practitioner asks questions about the    11. _____
client's customs and traditions. The practitioner is most likely seeking information about the impact of _____ on the client's function-
ing.

A.    unhealthy patterns
B.    self-talk
C.    interpersonal relationships
D.    cultural diversity

12) Each of the following is true of the intervention phase of social work,     12. _____
EXCEPT that it

A.    is focused on problems
B.    requires interviewing, recording, letter writing, and referral skills
C.    is guided by the principles of self-determination and acceptance
D.    results naturally from a thorough assessment

13) During a client interview, a practitioner is attempting to summarize         13. _____
what the client has just said, but the client gives signs that he does not agree
with the summary and intends to interrupt. The practitioner believes it is
important for the client to hear how the summary sounds in someone else's
words. In order to maintain his turn at speaking, the practitioner may want to

A.    raise an index finger
B.    raise his eyebrows
C.    speak more loudly
D.    stop all accompanying gestures and body movements

14) In Erikson's model of human development, the stage at which a child     14. _____
learns to meet the demands of society is

A. identity vs. role confusion
B. industry vs. inferiority
C. basic trust vs. mistrust
D. autonomy vs. shame and doubt

15) Generally, controlled experimental designs account for about _____     15. _____
percent of all social work research.

A. 5
B. 20
C. 35
D. 55

16) What is the term for a social work process that brings an intervention     16. _____
to a close?

A. Recognizing success
B. Integrating gains
C. Terminating the relationship
D. Expanding opportunities

17) Which of the following is an example of primary prevention for mental     17. _____
illness?

A. Crisis intervention
B. Parent-child communication training
C. Psychotherapy
D. Teacher referrals to social workers of children targeted by bullies

18) Which of the following is an example of a closed question?     18. _____

A. How do you think you can, as you've said, 'Come more alive?'
B. Of all the problems we've discussed, which bothers you the most?
C. What is your relationship with your family?
D. What kinds of things do you find yourself longing for?

19) Over time, adult personalities are likely to change in each of the fol-     19. _____
lowing ways, EXCEPT becoming more

A. candid
B. dependable
C. receptive to the company of others
D. accepting of hardship

20)    Which of the following BEST describes the mission of social work?    20. _____

A.    Meeting client needs while influencing social institutions to become more responsive to people
B.    Helping clients negotiate an often complex and difficult network of services
C.    Constantly responding and adapting to social changes in micro and macro environments
D.    Identifying programs and connecting clients to needed services

21)    Numerous studies have been conducted to determine which factors in    21. _____
a client/helping professional relationship are consistently related to positive outcomes. Which of the following is/are NOT one of these conditions?

A.    A relationship analogous to doctor/patient
B.    Empathy and positive regard
C.    A working alliance
D.    Transference and countertransference

22)    A person who donates anonymously to a favorite charity is most likely    22. _____
driven by what Maslow called

A.    intrinsic motivation
B.    extrinsic motivation
C.    affective habituation
D.    self-actualization

23)    According to the NASW code of ethics, sexual contact between practi-    23. _____
tioners and former clients is

A.    strongly discouraged under any circumstances
B.    discouraged, but considered acceptable if it occurs two years or more after the professional relationship has been terminated
C.    grounds for expulsion from the social work profession
D.    a private matter whose nature is left entirely up to the practitioner and the client

24)    During an unstructured interview with a client, a practitioner generally    24. _____
focuses on

A.    discovering the presenting problem
B.    confronting erroneous self-talk
C.    giving reflective responses that elicit more information
D.    a prescribed list of screening questions

25) Process recording is an assessment technique that is most often used in     25. _____

A.   clinical settings
B.   family sculpting
C.   one-on-one interviews
D.   group sessions

26) The NASW's stance on bartering with clients, rather than simply     26. _____
charging fees for service, includes the opinion that social workers should

   I.     participate in barter in only in very limited circumstances
   II.    ensure that such arrangements are an accepted practice among
          professionals in the local community
   III.   propose bartering if it is clear the client will be unable to pay
          for services
   IV.    never barter with clients under any circumstances

A.   I only
B.   I and II
C.   I, II and III
D.   IV only

                                                                                27. _____

27) Etiquette, customs, and minor regulations are examples of

A.   mores
B.   norms
C.   ethics
D.   folkways

28) A practitioner working in the Adlerian model is likely to use each of     28. _____
the following as an assessment instrument, EXCEPT

A.   personality inventories
B.   ecomaps
C.   lifestyle inventories
D.   early childhood recollections

29) Which of the following information would typically be solicited at the     29. _____
LATEST point in an intake interview?

A.   educational history
B.   family/marital/sexual history
C.   vocational history
D.   past interventions or service requests

30)    According to conflict theorists, the "hidden curriculum" of schools          30. _____

A.    serves to transmit different cultural values
B.    encourages social integration
C.    often results in self-fulfilling prophecy
D.    perpetuates existing social inequalities

31)    The high value placed on individual freedom in American society has          31. _____
arguably produced each of the following, EXCEPT

A.    a cultural paradox
B.    an environmental dilemma
C.    unfair economic competition
D.    a *caveat emptor* ("let the buyer beware") approach to the market
economy

32)    One model of the relationship between helping professionals and cli-          32. _____
ents emphasizes the social influence of professionals in counseling roles. To
be effective, practitioners in the counseling role can draw on a power base that
arises out of the relationship with the client. In client relationships, the power
base that is typically LEAST helpful for the practitioner is known as _____
_____ power.

A.    referent
B.    expert
C.    legitimate
D.    reward

33)    In social work, experimental research designs          33. _____

A.    are the most commonly conducted form of social work research
B.    obligate the researcher to offer a treatment to a control group as soon
as possible after the study is terminated
C.    are usually single-system designs
D.    are generally free of ethical concerns if the research is conducted well

34)    The term "social stratification" refers to social inequality that is          34. _____

A.    differential
B.    structured
C.    institutionally sanctioned
D.    imperceptible

35) To a practitioner working from the behavioral perspective, the most important feature of good relationships is

35. _____

A. effective coping behaviors
B. freedom from conflict
C. complementary needs
D. well-established boundaries

36) In an initial interview, it is common for clients to

36. _____

A. break down emotionally
B. describe problems in a way that minimizes their own contributions to them
C. disclose very personal information and emotions
D. be someone other than the person who has arranged the interview

37) Which of the following is NOT a trend in the use of family approaches in direct social work practice?

37. _____

A. Increased attention on the family as an isolated system
B. Increased attention to family diversity
C. The use of a variety of social science theoretical approaches
D. The use of multiple intervention models

38) The process whereby a client's place past feelings or attitudes toward significant people in their lives onto their social work practitioner is known as

38. _____

A. transference
B. denial
C. countertransference
D. projection

39) Social desirability bias often causes people to

39. _____

A. make appraisals of others that are based on their social functioning rather than their effectiveness in other roles
B. attribute their successes to skill, while blaming external factors for failures
C. modify their responses to surveys or interviews based on what they think are desirable responses
D. focus on the style of their interactions with others, rather than the substance

40)     A social worker attends an evening anniversary party at which she has     40. _____
consumed some alcohol, which she rarely drinks.  She doesn't think she is
literally drunk, but would acknowledge feeling slightly tipsy and perhaps not
in full command of herself.  When she arrives at home later, she listens to a
message from a client that was left on her answering machine while she was
out.  The client, with whom she has met several times, is feeling lonely and
desperate because of the recent loss of his wife to cancer.  The social worker
wants to help.  She should

A.     return the call immediately and try to counsel the client
B.     return the call immediately and explain that she is unable to help right
now, but will call first thing tomorrow
C.     avoid contacting the client until she has recovered her ability to perform up to her usual professional standards and judgement
D.     contact a trusted colleague, give him or her the relevant information,
and ask that he or she try to counsel the client over the phone

41)     During an assessment interview, a practitioner asks a client: "What     41. _____
kinds of feelings do you have when this happens to you?"  The practitioner is
trying to identify the _____ associated with the problem.

A.     affect and mood states
B.     secondary gains
C.     overt behaviors or motoric responses
D.     internal dialogue

42)     Hospital social workers typically engage in each of the following types     42. _____
of interventions or practice, EXCEPT

A.     crisis intervention
B.     discharge planning
C.     long-term counseling
D.     group work

43)     For social work practitioners, symptoms of "burnout" on the job typi-     43. _____
cally include each of the following, EXCEPT

A.     feeling unable to accomplish goals
B.     emotional exhaustion
C.     chronic worry
D.     a feeling of detachment from clients and work

44) When a case manager reaches the point in service coordination during which he makes a referral, he has assumed the role of

44. _____

A. evaluator
B. broker
C. advocate
D. planner

45) A practitioner encounters a situation in which his own personal values conflict with a client's. In this instance, the practitioner is expected to engage in

45. _____

A. peer review
B. value suspension
C. legal consultation
D. value clarification

46) Among the following American groups, the women who have the greatest risk of HIV infection are

46. _____

A. white
B. African American
C. Native American
D. Hispanic

47) The trend in school social work has been a gradual shift toward an emphasis on the _____ perspective.

47. _____

A. behavioral
B. input-based
C. ecological
D. psychiatric

48) The success of client-written logs as an assessment tool may depend on the client's motivation to keep a log. Which of the following is LEAST likely to help motivate a client to keep a log?

48. _____

A. Establishing a clear rationale or purpose for keeping the log
B. Establishing negative consequences if the client fails to make log entries
C. Adapting the log type to the client's abilities to self-monitor
D. Involving the client in discussing and analyzing the log

49)     The social work value of *empathy* is defined as a practitioner's capacity to          49. _____

A.     imagine oneself in another's situation
B.     feel compassion for a person who is in distress
C.     convince a person that things will get better
D.     make a person recognize his/her own inner strength

50)     Focusing on a client's positive assets and strengths during an assessment interview          50. _____

    I.     emphasizes the wholeness of the client system, rather than simply the problematic aspects
    II.     gives a practitioner information about potential problems that might arise during an intervention
    III.     helps convey to the client that they have internal resources that may prove useful
    IV.     risks skewing the effectiveness of an intervention by taking the focus off the presenting problem

A.     I and III
B.     I, II and III
C.     III only
D.     I, II, III and IV

51)     A hospital social worker is meeting with an 86-year-old man who suffers from Alzheimer's disease. His symptoms thus far have consisted largely of incidents of forgetfulness, and he has shown no signs of dementia or violence. The client's daughter, who has recently succeeded in having her father grant her a power of attorney over his affairs. When the social worker asks questions of the client, the daughter repeated breaks in and attempts to answer for him, though he appears to be lucid. When the social worker asks to speak to the client alone, the daughter refuses. The social worker should          51. _____

A.     suspect a case of elder abuse and contact the adult protective services agency to look into it
B.     pretend to leave, and then attempt to interview the man when the daughter leaves the room
C.     suspect that the daughter may have suffered abuse at the hands of her father and adult protective services to look into it
D.     suspect a case of elder abuse and contact local law enforcement authorities

52)    Which of the following is a key element of the case management para-    52. _____
digm?

A.    A focus on improving the quality and accessibility of resources
B.    A focus on developing vocational adjustment
C.    The selection of interventions based on empirical research
D.    Rational-emotive therapy

53)    Of the following health problems, each affects the elderly to a greater    53. _____
extent than other age groups.  The one that leads by the greatest percentage is

A.    cancer
B.    stroke
C.    heart disease
D.    Alzheimer's disease

54)    Approximately _____ of all direct practice interventions are    54. _____
terminated because of unanticipated situational factors.

A.    an eighth
B.    a quarter
C.    half
D.    three-quarters

55)    Social factors that increase the risk for suicide include each of the fol-    55. _____
lowing, EXCEPT that the person

A.    lives alone
B.    has repeatedly rejected support
C.    has no ongoing therapeutic relationship
D.    is married

56)    Practitioners are generally considered to have an ethical obligation to    56. _____
do each of the following, EXCEPT

A.    remain aware of their own values
B.    seek to learn about the diverse cultural backgrounds of their clients
C.    avoid imposing their values on clients
D.    refer clients whose values strongly differ from their own

57)    Studies of young people who join urban gangs suggests that most of-    57. _____
ten, people join gangs because of a need for a(n)

A.    peer group
B.    outlet for pent-up aggression and frustration
C.    surrogate family
D.    vehicle for criminal activity

58)    After terminating a working relationship with a social worker, a client          58. _____
joins the local chapter of Alcoholics Anonymous.  In doing so, she is attempting to

A.    form new therapeutic relationships
B.    prolong treatment
C.    maintain gains
D.    generalize gains

59)    A key concept of narrative therapy is the idea that          59. _____

A.    clients often construct one-dimensional stories that don't tell the whole
truth
B.    clearly naming a problem or disorder is the first step in solving it
C.    problems are inseparable from the person
D.    interventions are narrowly targeted to "revisions" of specific passages
within the story

60)    The creation of social service programs typically accomplishes each of          60. _____
the following, EXCEPT

A.    prevention
B.    enhancement
C.    retrenchment
D.    remediation

61)    The most significant health problem facing Native Americans today is          61. _____

A.    tuberculosis
B.    alcoholism
C.    heart disease
D.    diabetes

62)    Which of the following is NOT one of the six "core values" that is          62. _____
cited in the preamble to the NASW's code of ethics?

A.    Service
B.    Confidentiality
C.    Integrity
D.    Importance of human relationships

63)    Each of the following is a guideline for a practitioner's participation in     63. _____
crisis intervention procedures, EXCEPT

A.    expressing empathy by saying things such as "I understand"
B.    asking the client to describe the event
C.    letting the client talk for as long as he or she likes without
interruption
D.    asking the client to describe his or her reactions and responses

64)    A practitioner has begun to work with clients in one-on-one settings.     64. _____
He thinks perhaps self-disclosure would be a good way to establish a solid,
caring relationship with his clients.  He should remember that in working with
clients professionally, there will always be a tension between the competing
forces of self-disclosure and

A.    candor
B.    liability
C.    reciprocity
D.    privacy

65)    From an ethical standpoint, practitioners may     65. _____

    I.    accept a referral fee
    II.    refer a client to a single referral source
    III.    use a place of employment, such as a social services agency, to
        recruit clients for their own private practice
    IV.    refer clients only if their problems fall outside the practitioner's
        area of competence

A.    I  and II
B.    II only
C.    II, III and IV
D.    I, II, III and IV

66)    According to Carol H. Meyer's widely used model of social work as-     66. _____
sessment, the first step in the assessment process is

A.    evaluation
B.    inferential thinking
C.    problem definition
D.    exploration

67) What is the term for the theory that explains how people generate ex-  67. _____
planations for the behaviors of others?

A.    Attribution theory
B.    Stereotyping
C.    Thematic apperception
D.    Implicit personality theory

68) The most important professional risk associated with amalgamating  68. _____
groups under very broad headings or labels, such as "Asian American," is that

A.    these terms are considered derogatory by many people
B.    most immigrants to this country proudly insist on being referred to as
simply "American"
C.    many people resent being folded in to a larger group for the purpose of
classification
D.    the label may obscure significant differences in the culture and experiences of individuals or subgroups within the larger category

69) Before entering a social work field placement program, prospective  69. _____
students are ethically entitled to know

        I.     dismissal policies and procedures
        II.    employment prospects for graduates
        III.   the basis for performance evaluation
        IV.    names and theoretical perspectives of prospective supervisors

A.    I only
B.    I, II, and III
C.    III only
D.    I, II, III and IV

70) Of the steps involved in recruitment and training at human services  70. _____
organizations, the FIRST typically involves

A.    reference and background checks
B.    posting position announcements
C.    screening interviews
D.    developing a job description

71)     During an intake interview, a client generally avoids making eye con-     71. _____
tact with the practitioner.  Averting the eyes in this way is an example of the
_____ function of eye contact.

A.     monitoring
B.     expressive
C.     regulatory
D.     cognitive

72)     The educational success of American children and youth is highly cor-     72. _____
related to

A.     home schooling
B.     regional employment patterns
C.     family values
D.     race and ethnicity

73)     Which of the following techniques is a client-centered practitioner     73. _____
MOST likely to use?

A.     Response shaping
B.     Reflection
C.     Giving advice
D.     Analysis

74)     During a meeting with a client who has just ended his marriage after     74. _____
twelve years, the client insists repeatedly that everything is fine.  No matter
what the practitioner asks or tries to suggest, the response is the same.  The
client is engaging in the facial management technique known as

A.     neutralizing
B.     masking
C.     intensifying
D.     deintensifying

75)     A practitioner is considering a dual relationship with a client.  Before     75. _____
forming such a relationship, the practitioner should consider

        I.      divergent responsibilities
        II.     incompatible expectations
        III.    the power differential
        IV.     referring the client to another practitioner

A.     I and II
B.     I, II and III
C.     II, III and IV
D.     I, II, III and IV

# KEY (CORRECT ANSWERS)

| | | | | |
|---|---|---|---|---|
| 1. | A | | 41. | A |
| 2. | C | | 42. | C |
| 3. | C | | 43. | C |
| 4. | D | | 44. | B |
| 5. | D | | 45. | B |
| | | | | |
| 6. | C | | 46. | B |
| 7. | B | | 47. | C |
| 8. | B | | 48. | B |
| 9. | C | | 49. | A |
| 10. | B | | 50. | B |
| | | | | |
| 11. | D | | 51. | A |
| 12. | A | | 52. | A |
| 13. | C | | 53. | C |
| 14. | B | | 54. | C |
| 15. | A | | 55. | D |
| | | | | |
| 16. | B | | 56. | D |
| 17. | B | | 57. | C |
| 18. | B | | 58. | C |
| 19. | C | | 59. | A |
| 20. | A | | 60. | C |
| | | | | |
| 21. | A | | 61. | B |
| 22. | A | | 62. | B |
| 23. | A | | 63. | A |
| 24. | C | | 64. | D |
| 25. | C | | 65. | B |
| | | | | |
| 26. | B | | 66. | D |
| 27. | D | | 67. | A |
| 28. | A | | 68. | D |
| 29. | B | | 69. | B |
| 30. | D | | 70. | D |
| | | | | |
| 31. | A | | 71. | C |
| 32. | D | | 72. | D |
| 33. | B | | 73. | B |
| 34. | B | | 74. | A |
| 35. | A | | 75. | B |
| | | | | |
| 36. | B | | | |
| 37. | A | | | |
| 38. | A | | | |
| 39. | C | | | |
| 40. | C | | | |

# EXAMINATION SECTION
## TEST 1

**Directions:** Each question or incomplete statement is followed by several suggested answers or completions. Select the one that BEST answers the question or completes the statement. *PRINT THE LETTER OF THE CORRECT ANSWER IN THE SPACE AT THE RIGHT.*

1) For children, divorce has been identified as a risk factor for

    I.     being abused
    II.    substance abuse
    III.   lower academic achievement
    IV.   criminal involvement

A.    I and II
B.    II and III
C.    II, III and IV
D.    I, II, III and IV

1._____

2) In formulating useful goals with clients, a social worker is guided by several principles. Which of the following is NOT one of these principles?

A.    Goal formulation is often delimited by the purpose of the agency, and may necessitate referral.
B.    It is necessary to designate a target person whose condition is to be changed or maintained.
C.    Goals should always be stated positively—in terms of *doing* something, rather than simply *not doing* something.
D.    The establishment of a time frame for achievement is counterproductive in the formulation of goals.

2._____

3) In selecting members for group social work, homogeneity will prove most important regarding

A.    intelligence
B.    ethnicity
C.    age, especially for young children
D.    common interests

3._____

4) A practitioner will probably NOT work well with diverse populations if he

A.    believes he is free from any racist attitudes, beliefs, or feelings
B.    is comfortable with the differences between himself and clients
C.    is flexible in applying theories to specific situations
D.    is open to being challenged and teste

4._____

5)      "Non-verbal" messages of practitioners and clients refer to      5. _____

A.      statements that nobody should be permitted to make in an interpersonal relationship
B.      ideas and thoughts that are left unrevealed
C.      written or otherwise documented statements about problems, recommendations, and solutions
D.      the entire range of facial and body expressions that communicate feelings

6)      During an assessment interview, a social worker should usually avoid      6. _____
asking _____ questions.

A.      "why"
B.      probing
C.      open-ended
D.      closed-ended

7)      Common goals of foster parent organizations include each of the following, EXCEPT      7. _____

A.      elevating the public's regard for foster care
B.      the facilitation of adoption by foster parents
C.      influencing legislation that concerns children and natural parents
D.      disseminating information among foster parents

8)      "Homeostasis" is a concept that has been traditionally used to describe      8. _____
how

A.      organisms maintain a constant external environment,
B.      organisms keep themselves stable through self-regulating mechanisms
C.      humans tend to form groups or tribes around food supplies
D.      humans display a broad but fixed range of behaviors

9)      A practitioner welcomes a client at the door of his office by saying,      9. _____
"Come in and sit down." He gestures to the room and the chair inside. This
gesture is a _____ of the practitioner's verbal message

A.      complementation
B.      repetition
C.      regulation
D.      contradiction

10) In interviewing clients, practitioners should be careful to avoid non-verbal behaviors that are generally considered to be negative. These gestures include each of the following, EXCEPT

A. body rotated slightly away from the client
B. crossing and recrossing legs
C. slightly backward body lean
D. frequent eye contact

10. _____

11) When a practitioner asks himself: "Is our agency's program doing what it had hoped to do?" he is asking himself a _____ question.

A. client outcome assessment
B. intervention effectiveness
C. process evaluation
D. program evaluation

11. _____

12) Of the following, which provides the BEST definition of the process of social work?

A. A distinct set of skills that allow the worker to tap into a variety of skills to improve conditions surrounding the client system
B. A helping activity undertaken to improve social functioning through direct involvement with the client or the systems that impact him
C. A series of programmed interventions designed to shape the client and his environment
D. A professional service to people in need who are unwilling or unable to act in their own best interests

12. _____

13) Which of the following is NOT a basic component of social work "competence," as defined by the NASW?

A. Accepting responsibility or employment only on the basis of existing competence or the intention to acquire the necessary competence.
B. Not allowing their personal problems, psychosocial distress, legal problems, substance abuse, or mental health difficulties to interfere with professional judgment and performance.
C. Basing practice on recognized knowledge, including empirically based knowledge, relevant to social work and social work ethics.
D. Striving to become and remain proficient in professional practice and the performance of professional functions.

13. _____

14)    For practitioners who hope to draw upon Piaget's theory of cognitive     14. _____
development in their work with clients, probably the biggest shortcoming of
his theory is that it

A.    does not examine any cognitive development beyond adolescence
B.    pigeonholes clients into distinct categories
C.    excludes questions of morality
D.    does not examine behavioral components of cognitions

15)    Which of the following is true of institutional discrimination?     15. _____

A.    It is often concealed through legal maneuverings.
B.    It is limited to large, formal organizations.
C.    It is woven into the fabric of society.
D.    It is a construction of the elite.

16)    In the solution-focused model of intervention, the best way to solve     16. _____
problems is to

A.    discover when the client is not having a problem, and then build on
that
B.    understand the goals and ambitions of the client
C.    determine the function that the problematic behavior serves for the cli-
ent
D.    define the problem in terms of the client's external environment

17)    A child in Piaget's preoperational stage     17. _____

    I.    is capable of altruism
    II.    uses transductive reasoning
    III.    is egocentric
    IV.    derives thought from sensation and movement

A.    I and II
B.    I, III and IV
C.    II and III
D.    I, II, III and IV

18)    Which of the following is NOT a primary human motive?     18. _____

A.    Desire for competence
B.    Avoidance of pain
C.    Thirst
D.    Hunger

19)     Summarizing clients' statements is an active listening strategy that     19. _____
is often useful for distilling statements into their important elements.  The
FIRST step in developing a good summarization of client statements during an
interview is to

A.      covertly restating the message or series of messages to yourself
B.      listening for the presence of "feeling" words
C.      ask the client to summarize for herself
D.      identify any relevant patterns themes, or multiple elements

20)     Each of the following is considered to be a desirable outcome of an     20. _____
initial interview with an applicant for social services, EXCEPT that the applicant

A.      leaves confident of working with the practitioner or case manager
toward a satisfactory solution
B.      understands his/her responsibilities in the treatment or intervention
C.      feels free to express him/herself
D.      feeling some rapport with the practitioner or case manager

21)     When counseling clients, social work practitioners will generally be     21. _____
effective if they

        I.      are able to recognize and accept their own power
        II.     can focus on the present moment
        III.    remain in the active process of developing their own counsel
                ing style
        IV.     are not afraid to offer advice

A.      I and III
B.      I, II and III
C.      II, III and IV
D.      I, II, III and IV

22)     According to the NASW's code of ethics, social workers who have     22. _____
direct knowledge of a social work colleague's incompetence should FIRST

A.      consult with that colleague when feasible and assist the colleague in
taking remedial action
B.      take action through the appropriate channels established by the employers or agency
C.      notify the NASW and any appropriate licensing and regulating bodies
D.      solicit the opinion of at least one other social worker with approximately equal qualifications and responsibilities to determine a course of action

23)     Countertransference, if recognized by the practitioner, can be a useful          23. _____
element in a client relationship.  Often, however, it is not helpful—or even
hurtful.  Hurtful forms typically involve each of the following, EXCEPT
countertransference that

A.      causes a practitioner to emit subtle clues that "lead" the client
B.      causes a practitioner to adopt the role the client wants us to play in his
or her traditional "script"
C.      is used at a distance to generate empathy for the client
D.      blinds a practitioner from an important area of exploration

24)     During any intervention, a social worker's final activities are aimed at          24. _____
_____ in the client's everyday functioning.

        I.      stabilizing success
        II.     generalizing outcomes
        III.    preventing recidivism
        IV.     restricting options

A.      I and II
B.      I and III
C.      II, III and IV
D.      I, II, III and IV

25)     In the documentation and report writing phase of assessment, a service          25. _____
coordinator's documentation responsibilities usually consist of

A.      social histories and intake summaries
B.      medical and social histories
C.      staff notes and mental status examinations
D.      intake summaries and staff notes

26)     A social work practitioner is MOST likely to increase the chances of          26. _____
his clients' connecting with the appropriate services when he

A.      refers clients to other more skilled professionals in the hope that these
professionals will be able to determine how best to meet the clients' needs
B.      promotes self determination by providing a list of agencies in the area
and allowing the clients to decide who can best meet their needs
C.      acquire expertise in as many areas of social work practice as possible,
in order to directly provide needed services
D.      becomes knowledgeable about programs and providers available, and
actively brokers needed services

27) One explanation for the steady increase in the divorce rate in the United States is that industrialization and urbanization led to a change in the roles played by family members. This explanation is consistent with the _____ perspective.

27. _____

A. symbolic interaction
B. structural functionalist
C. subcultural
D. social conflict

28) One of the most significant criticisms about the use of strategic planning in human services organizations is that it

28. _____

A. leaves many stakeholders in the dark about the organization's objectives
B. limits responsiveness to changing community needs
C. erodes employee morale and commitment to the organizational mission
D. is often too abstract to be useful in day-to-day management

29) The way in which a practitioner conceptualizes a client's problem configuration is known as

29. _____

A. conceptualization
B. the internal working model
C. mental set
D. framing

30) Significant factors that have contributed to the changing nature of American families since the 1970s include

30. _____

I. an increase in births outside marriage
II. a greater number of remarriages in which partners bring children from previous relationships
III. altered gender role expectations
IV. an increase in the number of partners who divorce or separate

A. I, II and IV
B. I and III
C. III only
D. I, II, III and IV

31) Culture maintains boundaries in each of the following ways, EXCEPT    31. _____
by

A.    instilling a sense of genuineness about the alternatives peculiar to a
society
B.    constructing symbols and meanings
C.    limiting the ranges of acceptable behavior and attitudes
D.    establishing the tendency for people to think of other societies as infe-
rior

32) The solution-focused perspective defines a client who describes a    32. _____
problem but isn't willing to work on solving it as a

A.    resistor
B.    complainant
C.    dam-builder
D.    procrastinator

33) During an assessment interview, a practitioner is trying to identify the    33. _____
range of problems that a client is experiencing. Which of the following communication skills is most appropriately used for this purpose?

A.    Open-ended questions
B.    Closed-ended questions
C.    Confrontation
D.    Interpretation

34) Social workers who have unresolved personal conflicts should    34. _____

A.    recognize that their problems may interfere with the effectiveness and
avoid activities or responses that could harm a client
B.    repress any anxiety-provoking issues in their own lives before attempting to work with others
C.    use their experience to lead clients in a mutual resolution of these
problems
D.    resolve these conflicts before planning a client intervention—and ide-
ally, before meeting the client at all.

35) Based largely on the understanding that all people break rules at one    35. _____
time or another, _____ theorists make the assumption that
what we call "deviant" is actually part of an overall pattern of normality.

A.    labeling
B.    social Darwinism
C.    conflict
D.    order

36) Rural clients tend to evaluate social workers on the basis of     36. \_\_\_\_\_

A.     the level of education the worker has achieved
B.     help delivered or problems solved
C.     the type of intervention used
D.     areas of specialization

37) A client is having trouble at work. He tells the practitioner: "I have a     37. \_\_\_\_\_
hard time relating to authority figures." He is describing his problem behavior

A.     in a way that places responsibility squarely on himself
B.     covertly
C.     in nonbehavioral terms
D.     without any affective cues

38) The practice of limiting a client's right to self-determination in order to     38. \_\_\_\_\_
protect him or her from self-harm is known in social work as

A.     gatekeeping
B.     paternalism
C.     delimiting behavior
D.     proxy

39) Which of the following is LEAST likely to be a symptom of stress?     39. \_\_\_\_\_

A.     Emotional instability
B.     Lethargy
C.     Sleep problems
D.     Digestive problems

40) In the traditional clinical model of school social work, a practitioner     40. \_\_\_\_\_
was probably LEAST likely to execute the role of

A.     enabler
B.     consultant
C.     supporter
D.     advocate

41) When advocating for a client, the first attempt at advocacy should     41. \_\_\_\_\_
always be

A.     a legal challenge
B.     a formal appeal
C.     temperate persuasion
D.     widely spread publicity about the client's case

42)    During regular meetings with his practitioner, a client has the tendency     42. _____
to ascribe the achievements of others to good luck or easy tasks, while assum-
ing his failures to be due to a lack of ability or experience.  The client's thinking is a phenomenon known as

A.    fundamental attribution bias
B.    the Hawthorne effect
C.    self-serving bias
D.    the halo effect

43)    The responsibilities of social work intern instructors typically include     43. _____
each of the following, EXCEPT

A.    clearly stating roles and responsibilities of interns in the field
B.    clearly stating the roles and responsibilities of site supervisors
C.    acting on site supervisors' recommendations following a negative
intern evaluation
D.    developing clear field placement policies

44)    A teenage client has been having problems in school—he is constantly     44. _____
being disciplined for being disruptive.  Discussions with the client reveal that
even though he has lost several privileges at school, he is reluctant to give up
his disruptive behavior because of the attention it brings in from his peers.
The attention of the client's peers is an example of a(n)

A.    secondary gain
B.    behavioral consequence
C.    negative reinforcement
D.    cognitive dissonance

45)    Which of the following is NOT a typical purpose of client self-moni-     45. _____
toring?

A.    To shift the burden of decision-making onto the client
B.    To validate the accuracy of the client's reports during interviews
C.    To test out hunches about the problem
D.    To help practitioner and client gain information about what actually
occurs with respect to the problem in real-life situations

46)    Which of the following is a "lower-order" human need, as identified in     46. _____
Maslow's hierarchy?

A.    Belonging
B.    Status
C.    Fulfillment
D.    Security

47)     Gene, a social worker, finds himself wanting to solve his client's prob-     47. _____
lems with alcohol dependency, which are similar to problems Gene's own son
went through several years ago.  Gene gives advice and is frustrated when the
client doesn't follow through on his suggestions.  Gene's emotional reactions
to his client are based on

A.     countertransference
B.     nurturing
C.     transference
D.     empathy

48)     In the termination phase of treatment, strategies for maintaining client     48. _____
gains may include each of the following, EXCEPT

A.     increasing the client's sense of mastery through realistic praise
B.     anticipating and planning for possible future difficulties
C.     highlighting and specifying the client's role in maintaining change
D.     teaching the client to deal with problems that underlie a coping pattern

49)     After receiving a notification about a 10-year-old boy's underperfor-     49. _____
mance at school, a social worker has tried twice to arrange a meeting with the
boy's 28-year-old mother, who works long hours as a waitress and has sole
responsibility for his care.  Both times, the mother has cancelled the meeting
at the last minute, citing sudden work conflicts.

        The social worker schedules an in-home visit to the boy's family—but
when he arrives, he is told by the boy that the mother is at work.  The child's
grandmother also lives in the home, but is bedridden, and the boy and his
sister help care for her.  The family's apartment is in disarray, with dirty dishes
stacked in the sink and on the stovetop.  Laundry is strewn about in wrinkled
piles.  The social worker observes no alcohol in the house, and the grandmother, who is cooperative, says that her daughter doesn't drink, and never has.

        As the social worker continues to monitor this family, he should be
especially alert for signs of

A.     a personality disorder on the part of the mother
B.     child abuse
C.     substance abuse
D.     child neglect

50)     Within practice settings that call upon the practitioner's knowledge and     50. _____
skill at all levels of the organization, the social work profession is considered
to be a(n) _____ discipline.

A.     primary
B.     secondary
C.     collegial
D.     ancillary

51)     Among gays and lesbians, stress and a lack of emotional support have     51. _____
been shown to contribute to

A.     high rates of alcoholism
B.     promiscuity
C.     identity fragmentation
D.     erratic employment patterns

52)     An elderly client is particularly concerned about being "bothered"     52. _____
all the time by a social work practitioner who frequently visits her home. To
avoid too much discomfort on the part of the client, the practitioner has the
client sign several blank consent forms so that her medical history can be
sent to several agencies that might offer supportive services. In this case, the
worker has

A.     violated the principle of informed consent
B.     hit upon a key strategy for avoiding burnout
C.     demonstrated ignorance of the eligibility rules for most service agen-
cies
D.     found an ethical strategy for streamlining an often frustrating bureau-
cracy

53)     The most common diagnoses for people who complete suicide are     53. _____

A.     schizophrenia and substance abuse
B.     depressive illness and borderline personality disorder
C.     depressive illness and alcoholism
D.     schizophrenia and chronic metabolic disease

54)     The mother of a 14-year-old girl telephoned crisis services, telling the     54. _____
worker that her son had just locked and barricaded himself in his room. Earlier, she had overheard a conversation between the boy and his girlfriend that
was clearly a fight. She is concerned because the boy had tried to overdose
after the end of an earlier relationship.
        A worker was immediately dispatched to the residence. After a
lengthy conversation in which the worker successfully established rapport
with the boy, the boy agreed to let the worker in.
        Thus far, crisis services and the worker have followed the formula of
Roberts's Seven-Stage Crisis Intervention Model. As a next step, the worker
will attempt to

A.     explore alternatives to suicide, such as inpatient or outpatient services
B.     identify and validate the boy's emotions
C.     develop an action plan with the boy
D.     have the boy identify what he views as the major problem or problems

55) The primary goal of crisis intervention can best be described as 55. _____

A. protecting the client from a situation in which he or she has become more likely to experience a traumatic event than other people
B. helping the client to identify and endure the long-term consequences of a traumatic event
C. protecting a client from self-harm following a traumatic event
D. helping the client to identify and cope with the sense of "disequilibrium" in the aftermath of a trauma

56) A practitioner discovers that a client is behaving in a way that is seriously damaging both to himself and a close relative. While respecting the concept of self-determination and confidentiality, the practitioner should 56. _____

A. warn the client that he (the practitioner) has an obligation to divulge the client's behavior to the appropriate agency or authority, and then do so
B. attempt to dissuade the client from further engaging in behavior that is harmful
C. immediately alert the authorities
D. refer the client to a social services worker who has more experience in this specific type of behavior

57) In order to serve effectively in rural communities, social work practitioners would most likely need to incorporate the concepts of _____ _____ into their practice. 57. _____

A. nature and seasonal fluctuation
B. self-reliance and mutual aid
C. land and ownership
D. religion and spirituality

58) Which of the following is NOT typically included in a service agreement between a practitioner and a client? 58. _____

A. Description of the agency's programs and services
B. Fees for service or arrangements for reimbursement
C. Theoretical framework for the relationship
D. Time frames for the provision of services

59) From a legal perspective, case records 59. _____

A. belong to the practitioner who created them
B. belong to the client
C. belong to the agency at which they are physically held
D. are for the benefit of the client

60) A practitioner is speaking to a client via cellular phone. The practitio-    60. \_\_\_\_\_
ner should be aware that

    I.      there is a chance that the call could be intercepted by an unau
           thorized party
    II.    the client may not be in a private place
    III.   telephone conversations are not considered to be a public ser
           vice
    IV.   complete privacy cannot be assured

A.    I and II
B.    I, II, and IV
C.    III only
D.    I, II, III and IV

61) The basic assumptions underlying social work administration do NOT    61. \_\_\_\_\_
include the statement that

A.    each person who works within the agency should be considered a
stakeholder in agency outcomes
B.    administration is largely the process of securing and transforming
community resources
C.    the major contributions toward the improvement of administration
come from management itself
D.    the agency has the primary responsibility for the creation and control
of its own destiny

62) Most Asian Americans who are seeking assistance from a social work    62. \_\_\_\_\_
practitioner are looking for a professional who is

A.    nondirective
B.    problem-focused
C.    goal-oriented
D.    experiential in focus

63) Privileged communication is NOT    63. \_\_\_\_\_

A.    widely varying in state-to-state legal definitions
B.    usually waived if a third party is present
C.    particularly difficult to protect when working with married couples
D.    protected no matter what the risks involved

64)     In devising a treatment plan, a practitioner begins with client tasks that     64. _____
can be managed fairly easily and with some success, before moving on to the
larger issues that are causing problems.  In doing so, the practitioner is adher-
ing to the rule of

A.      successive approximations
B.      object orientation
C.      positive reinforcement
D.      mental set

65)     "Preparatory empathy" is a process that is used by a practitioner in     65. _____
order to

A.      insure against client deception
B.      streamline an intervention by figuring some things out in advance
C.      choose necessary resources or services
D.      make him more aware of issues or barriers that might be encountered

66)     The federal WIC program specifically targets the health and welfare of     66. _____

A.      abused children
B.      adoptive families
C.      pregnant women and newborn children
D.      unskilled laborers who have been injured on the job

67)     Of all Hispanics living the United States, those of Mexican descent ac-     67. _____
count for about _____ percent of the total.

A.      20
B.      40
C.      60
D.      80

68)     From her first few meetings with a client, a social work practitioner     68. _____
has begun to form an impression.  If the practitioner seeks out additional information that will help to confirm or deny her existing impressions, she will
be engaging in

A.      cognitive integration
B.      active perception
C.      offensive perception
D.      thematic apperception

69)     A social worker is using the person-in-environment (PIE) system of     69. _____
client assessment.  In describing the environmental problems that affect a
client's social functioning, the social worker will rely on six groupings of
social system problems. Which of the following is NOT one of the groupings
used in the PIE system?

A.      Economic/basic need
B.      Judicial/legal system
C.      Physical health
D.      Education and training

70)     Basic social work values that influence professional practice include     70. _____
each of the following, EXCEPT

A.      self-determination
B.      the inherent uniqueness of a person
C.      individualism
D.      the inherent worth and dignity of a person

71)     Which step in the listening process involves the assignment of mean-     71. _____
ing to a message?

A.      Encoding
B.      Attending
C.      Understanding
D.      Selecting

72)     Qualitative social work research     72. _____

A.      observes people in natural settings and focuses on the meaning they
assign to experiences.
B.      is analyzed through the use of bivariate methods
C.      details the past in order to understand present conditions
D.      compares statistics from number of cases

73)     When a worker attempts to "cement" a referral, she is attempting to     73. _____

A.      make sure the client is connected to the suggested resource
B.      make the working relationship into a strong enough bond that the cli-
ent will be sure to follow through
C.      use software or another evaluative tool that confirms the appropriate-
ness of the client to the proposed resource
D.      suggest to the client in advance that the referral will result in success

74) In working with a client, a practitioner is careful to avoid singling out    74. _____
one or two obvious client characteristics as the reason for everything the person does. The tendency to do this is known as

A.  stereotyping
B.  scripting
C.  over-attribution
D.  highballing

75) A group's sense of ethnic identity is affected by the    75. _____

    I.      degree to which the members' physical appearances differ from
           those in mainstream society
    II.    size of the group
    III.   amount of power the group has
    IV.   extent of assimilation

A.  I only
B.  I and III
C.  II and IV
D.  I, II, III and IV

# KEY (CORRECT ANSWERS)

| | | | | |
|---|---|---|---|---|
| 1. | D | | 41. | C |
| 2. | D | | 42. | A |
| 3. | C | | 43. | C |
| 4. | A | | 44. | A |
| 5. | D | | 45. | A |
| | | | | |
| 6. | A | | 46. | D |
| 7. | B | | 47. | A |
| 8. | B | | 48. | D |
| 9. | B | | 49. | D |
| 10. | D | | 50. | A |
| | | | | |
| 11. | D | | 51. | A |
| 12. | B | | 52. | A |
| 13. | B | | 53. | C |
| 14. | A | | 54. | D |
| 15. | C | | 55. | D |
| | | | | |
| 16. | A | | 56. | A |
| 17. | C | | 57. | B |
| 18. | A | | 58. | C |
| 19. | A | | 59. | B |
| 20. | B | | 60. | B |
| | | | | |
| 21. | B | | 61. | C |
| 22. | A | | 62. | A |
| 23. | C | | 63. | D |
| 24. | A | | 64. | A |
| 25. | D | | 65. | D |
| | | | | |
| 26. | D | | 66. | C |
| 27. | B | | 67. | C |
| 28. | D | | 68. | B |
| 29. | A | | 69. | C |
| 30. | D | | 70. | C |
| | | | | |
| 31. | A | | 71. | C |
| 32. | B | | 72. | A |
| 33. | A | | 73. | A |
| 34. | A | | 74. | C |
| 35. | A | | 75. | D |
| | | | | |
| 36. | B | | | |
| 37. | C | | | |
| 38. | B | | | |
| 39. | B | | | |
| 40. | D | | | |

# TEST 2

**Directions:** Each question or incomplete statement is followed by several suggested answers or completions. Select the one that BEST answers the question or completes the statement. *PRINT THE LETTER OF THE CORRECT ANSWER IN THE SPACE AT THE RIGHT.*

1) In the _____ style of conflict management, the parties attempt to separate themselves from the problem.

1. _____

A. cooperative
B. nonconfrontational
C. mediative
D. settlement

2) The purposes of staff notes, or progress notes, include

2. _____

    I.     recording client's responses to services
    II.    connecting a service to a key issue
    III.   describing client status
    IV.   providing direction for ongoing treatment

A. I only
B. I, II and III
C. III and IV
D. I, II, III and IV

3) A genogram is an assessment tool that

3. _____

A. involves DNA sampling
B. defers consideration of current family relationships
C. gives a picture of family relationships over at least three generations
D. uses statistical measures to calculate the probability of an intervention's success

4) Which of the following is NOT a belief of stage theorists?

4. _____

A. The progression of stages is biologically programmed.
B. Children pass through the same stages in the same sequence.
C. Stages are usually marked by age ranges.
D. As children progress through the stages, the differences between them are quantitative.

5)      During the opening phase of a client interview, the practitioner should      5. _____
probably spend most of his time and thoughts on

A.      self-disclosure
B.      negotiating a working contract
C.      interpreting behaviors
D.      explaining agency rules and protocols

6)      Behaviors commonly associated with substance abuse include      6. _____

        I.      a withdrawal from responsibility
        II.     unusual outbreaks of temper
        III.    abrupt changes in quality or output of work
        IV.     wearing sunglasses at inappropriate times

A.      I and II
B.      I, II and III
C.      II and IV
D.      I, II, III and IV

7)      Which of the following would a practitioner typically do FIRST in a      7. _____
problem assessment interview?

A.      Identify client coping skills
B.      Identify the range of client problems
C.      Prioritize and select issues and problems for discussion
D.      Identify consequences of problem behaviors

8)      A social worker's primary ethical duty is to      8. _____

A.      effect social justice
B.      promote the welfare of the client
C.      respect diversity
D.      avoid dependent relationships

9)      The person-centered model of human behavior views the major reason      9. _____
for maladjustment as a(n)

A.      failure to set a self-actualizing tendency in motion
B.      inability to establish unconditional positive regard
C.      incongruence between self-concept and experience
D.      unresolved childhood frustrations

10)    The person-in-environment (PIE) system of client assessment is a four-    10. _____
factor system.  Factor _____ provides a statement of the client's physical
health problems.

A.    I
B.    II
C.    III
D.    IV

11)    An adolescent client tells her social worker that she feels she is the    11. _____
only person in the world who has ever had such strong unrequited love for another person—the boy who sits next to her in geometry class.  The component
of adolescent egocentrism being enacted by the girl is the

A.    all-or-none fallacy
B.    imaginary audience
C.    questionable cause
D.    personal fable

12)    Research into interpersonal relationships suggests that women often    12. _____
build relationships through shared positive feelings, while men often build
relationships through

A.    shared activities
B.    shared opinions
C.    metacommunication
D.    impression management

13)    Which of the following is NOT typically a purpose of assessment?    13. _____

A.    To identify the controlling or contributing variables associated with a
client's problem
B.    To launch the first phase of treatment
C.    To educate and motivate the client by sharing views about the problem
D.    To plan effective interventions and strategies

14)    Persuading clients to abandon mistaken ways of thinking is a goal of    14. _____

A.    client-centered therapy
B.    operant conditioning
C.    cognitive therapy
D.    systematic desensitization

15)	A practitioner is creating an action plan with an adult client who has	15. _____
decided to leave his current job.  Typically, planning such a move requires
practitioner and client to move on to

A.	ensure that the work to be done fits an accepted model of treatment
B.	breaking large goals into component parts
C.	making the client aware of the full range of consequences
D.	ensure that this decision meets with the approval of the people who
will be affected by it

16)	Some of the information in an applicant's file comes from secondary	16. _____
sources.  Which of the following is NOT considered a secondary source?

A.	Applicant's family
B.	Referring agency
C.	School
D.	Current staff notes

17)	Self-disclosure is considered a "discretionary" response in discussions	17. _____
with clients, because it

A.	is not considered to be therapeutic
B.	is only used if the client requests it
C.	should be used carefully to avoid taking the focus off the client
D.	requires a familiarity with the client's worldview before it is used

18)	For a practitioner working from the family systems theory, symptoms	18. _____
of maladjustment in families are usually masked by

A.	the involvement and recommendations of professionals who were pre-
viously involved
B.	the presenting crisis or problem that initially brought the family into
contact with the agency
C.	abusive relationships
D.	environmental components in the family's community

19)	A school social worker is told that one of the kindergartners is running	19. _____
around, out of control, and disrupting the others at naptime.  As she attempts
to understand the problem, her FIRST step should be to

A.	arrange an interview with the school psychologist
B.	look into finding an alternative school placement
C.	systematically observe the child in the classroom to see how it is man-
aged
D.	contact the parents to inform them of the child's behavior problems

20)   What is the collective term applied to communication variables such as     20. _____
voice level, pitch, rate, and fluency of speech?

A.   Kinesics
B.   Paralinguistics
C.   Nonverbal messages
D.   Proxemics

21)   Although the terms *counseling* and *interviewing* are sometimes used     21. _____
interchangeably in social work, there are differences that should be noted.
Which of the following is NOT one of these differences.

A.   Interviewing is a responsibility that can be assumed by most practitioners or case managers.
B.   Interviewing is a more basic process for information gathering and
problem solving.
C.   Counseling is a more intensive and personal process.
D.   Counseling is often associated with nonprofessional workers, whereas
therapy used to indicate professional interventions.

22)   A social worker in the _____ role is conducting "mac-     22. _____
ro" practice.

   I.    manager
   II.   planner
   III.  case manager
   IV.   mediator

A.   I and II
B.   I, II and IV
C.   III only
D.   I, II, III and IV

                                                                              23. _____
23)   The final stage of Elisabeth Kubler-Ross's theory of how people
handle the knowledge of their impending death is known as

A.   denial
B.   bargaining
C.   anger
D.   acceptance

24)    Probably the most important factor in establishing a working alliance       24. _____
with a client is the

A.    client's belief about whether the practitioner attends and understands
B.    accuracy of the practitioner's assessment of the presenting problem(s)
C.    practitioner's effort to be empathetic
D.    client's initial willingness to change

25)    During the assessment phase, the practice of _____       25. _____
___ means that the practitioner and client are setting specific objectives.

A.    activating resources
B.    framing solutions
C.    defining the problem
D.    weighing alternatives

26)    Reflecting and paraphrasing are two active listening strategies often       26. _____
used by practitioners to help clients become more aware of the implications of
their own statements.  Basically the difference between reflecting and paraphrasing involves the difference between the

A.    client's words and the client's actions
B.    the emotional (affective) and factual (cognitive) content of messages
C.    way the client perceives the world and the way the world actually is
D.    way the client is expressing a message and the way it is being received
by the practitioner

27)    The process by which people shape social life by adapting to, negotiat-       27. _____
ing with, and changing social structures is known as

A.    determinism
B.    positivism
C.    human agency
D.    ideology

28)    Child welfare is a social work practice area that       28. _____

A.    focuses on issues, problems, and policies related to the well-being of
children
B.    administers school lunches and other benefit programs for low-income
children
C.    focuses on increasing the educational potential of children
D.    mainly works to broker adoptions

29)    The relationship between social work supervisors and supervisees,    29. _____
which parallels the relationship between social worker and client, has been described in terms of basic relational elements.  Which of the following is NOT
one of these?

A.    Caring
B.    Rapport
C.    Authority
D.    Trust

30)    The _____ model attributes the essential characteristics    30. _____
of consensus, cohesion, stability, reciprocity, and cooperation to society.

A.    evolutionary
B.    conflict
C.    order
D.    symbolic interaction

31)    Upholding rules, regulations and restrictions of a social services    31. _____
agency—which are not always best for the client—is a function of the social
worker's role known as

A.    gatekeeping
B.    spoilage
C.    advocacy
D.    bureaucratic blindness

32)    A social worker and her client have developed a long-range goal.  Now    32. _____
they are determining individual steps that will lead to the achievement of that
goal.  This is a process known as

A.    chunking
B.    prioritizing
C.    partializing
D.    contracting

33)    Community surveys, policy analyses, and case histories are examples    33. _____
of

A.    social studies
B.    ecomaps
C.    needs assessments
D.    genograms

34) In a social services agency that serves teenage runaways, an example    34. _____
of a direct service strategy would be

A.    organizing
B.    counseling
C.    gathering information
D.    planning

35) Compared to others in society, those with superior _____    35. _____
are more likely to support the status quo.

A.    educational achievement
B.    social locations
C.    value systems
D.    incomes

36) "Primary prevention" means    36. _____

A.    the severity and duration of a disease or disorder have been reduced
B.    clinical means have been used to provide treatment, such as crisis
intervention
C.    a disease or disorder is stopped at its source, and the cause is elimi-
nated
D.    the spread of a disease or disorder among people has been limited

37) Under normal circumstances it is considered acceptable practice for a    37. _____
social worker to disclose a client's confidential information to

I.      the practitioner's supervisor as it relates to the supervisory rela
        tionship
II.     professionals who are consulted about assessments or interven-
        tions
III.    third-party payers for the purpose of justifying treatment deci-
        sions
IV.     close family members for the purpose of developing under-
        standing of the client's particular difficulties

A.    I only
B.    I and II
C.    I, II and III
D.    I, II, III and IV

38) A client's feelings of powerlessness can be reduced when a social          38. _____
worker adopts each of the following roles, EXCEPT the role of

A.     resource consultant, who connects the client to goods and services
B.     advocate, who acts as the client's protector in social living matters
C.     sensitizer, who helps the client gain knowledge needed to solve prob-
lems
D.     educator, who facilitates the learning and skill development needed for
goal setting and task completion

39) The _____ model of human services organization          39. _____
management places the greatest value on maximizing the productivity of the
organization.

A.     internal process
B.     open-system
C.     rational goal
D.     human relations

40) During an interview, practitioner and client establish a goal for the cli-          40. _____
ent to use her time more efficiently at work and at home. This is an example
of a _____ goal.

A.     process
B.     survival
C.     treatment
D.     service

41) One reason people often confuse race and ethnicity is because they          41. _____

A.     are suspicious of people who are different from themselves
B.     are unaware that race is cultural and ethnicity is biological
C.     see cultural differences and define race in specific, often inaccurate
ways
D.     have met few people outside their own race

42) Dual relationships between a practitioner and a client, according to the          42. _____
NASW:

A.     should not be formed if there is any possibility for exploitation or po-
tential harm to the client
B.     are usually an unavoidable part of professional practice
C.     are generally acceptable if social workers take steps to protect clients
D.     are generally acceptable if social workers are careful to avoid legal
problems that could damage the status of the social work profession

43)    In a family intervention that implements the structural model, the fam-    43. _____
ily will be expected to

A.    submit to the direction of the practitioner
B.    solve their own problems
C.    shift their internal alliances
D.    shift blame to the external environment

44)    In diversion programs, social workers typically provide    44. _____

A.    case management services with probation officers in an attempt to
prevent recidivism
B.    consultation services about early-release programs for juvenile offend-
ers
C.    counseling services through a network of lay professionals
D.    crisis intervention or referral services aimed at avoiding imprisonment

45)    In hospital social work, an example of macropractice would be    45. _____

A.    connecting with community providers to maintain understanding of
community needs
B.    increasing health provider awareness of clients' home environment
C.    engaging clients in planning for their immediate future after discharge
D.    educating clients and families about the implications of a particular ill-
ness or disorder

46)    A client tells a practitioner that he is distraught over the end of his    46. _____
marriage and wishes he could "just go to sleep forever, be at peace, and not
have to feel this pain any more." The practitioner should

A.    assess whether the client is suicidal and intervene if necessary
B.    recognize that such statements are often merely a "cry for help" and
urge the client to focus on more practical issues
C.    contact the client's wife and determine whether there is a chance to
reconcile
D.    immediately commit the client to a psychiatric facility

47)    The presenting problems of most African American clients are rooted    47. _____
in

A.    genetics
B.    personality deficits
C.    stress from external systems
D.    unresolved family conflicts

48)     A solution-focused intervention would most likely involve the goal of     48. _____

A.     a first-order change in the client system
B.     behavioral continuity
C.     a perceptual shift from talking about problems to talking about how to solve them
D.     determining exactly how a problem came into being

49)     During an interview in which a client is being evaluated, the client     49. _____
should understand that the

A.     information gained during the interview may be the basis of a report on the client
B.     questions will not be upsetting to him/her
C.     interview will focus on the client's well-being
D.     he or she has implicitly entered into a service contract

50)     The _____ theory of rural social work asserts that there     50. _____
are distinct differences between rural and urban areas, and that the urban end
of the continuum is associated with social pathology.

A.     classical
B.     subcultural
C.     compositional
D.     determinist

51)     During the supervisory discussion of a client case, the FIRST topic of     51. _____
discussion should typically be

A.     client dynamics and problems
B.     alternative intervention strategies
C.     a tentative assessment or diagnosis
D.     selection of a general treatment approach

52)     The millions of Asian Americans living in the United States today     52. _____
represent a generally _____ population.

A.     prosperous
B.     culturally homogeneous
C.     mainstreamed
D.     heterogeneous

53) Most legal issues encountered by social work practitioners involve     53. _____

A. complaints of improper conduct
B. being sued for negligence or malpractice
C. being prosecuted for crimes
D. acting as witnesses in litigation

54) The initial recommended response to a client who is suicidal is     54. _____

A. hospitalization and observation
B. identifying the client's level of seriousness
C. problem-solving training
D. crisis intervention and a functional assessment of the suicidal behavior

55) The most common client reactions to the termination of direct social     55. _____
service include each of the following, EXCEPT

A. pride
B. ambivalence
C. satisfaction
D. denial

56) Most referrals to human service professionals are made by     56. _____

A. school systems
B. health care workers
C. the courts
D. word of mouth from friends or family members

57) The term "handicap" refers to a(n)

A. obstruction that prevents an interface between a disability and the en-     57. _____
vironment
B. an impairment that limits one's daily activities
C. inability to perform tasks at a level that is generally considered to be
socially acceptable
D. loss of use or function of an organ or bodily system

58)     When writing case notes, practitioners should always            58. _____

    I.      keep in mind that others may read the notes
    II.     compose them immediately after a client meeting
    III.    provide as much detail as possible
    IV.     use shorthand

A.      I and II
B.      II only
C.      I, II and III
D.      I, II, III and IV

59)     The most frequent cause of child death is                      59. _____

A.      physical abuse
B.      suicide
C.      being left unsupervised or alone for long periods of time
D.      automobile accidents

60)     Clients of social service agencies often disagree with either agency       60. _____
policies or a practitioner's actions, or both.  If a client demands to know why
a particular action was taken and perhaps reverse it, he or she is exercising a
right to

A.      confidentiality
B.      due process
C.      privileged information
D.      informed consent

61)     Content theories of human motivation argue that               61. _____

A.      most people dislike change
B.      external consequences determine behavior
C.      most people are affiliation-oriented
D.      internal needs lead to behavior

62)     Once a client's service needs are clear, a social worker often helps the      62. _____
client choose the most appropriate service and negotiates the terms of service
delivery.  Here, the social worker is acting in the role of

A.      broker
B.      consultant
C.      advocate
D.      coordinator

63)     When social work practitioners commit errors in working with gay,      63. _____
lesbian, and bisexual clients, these errors most often stem from the

A.      workers' own unconscious prejudices
B.      failure to recognize clients as homosexual, due to a lack of identifying
characteristics
C.      identification of client problems as being caused by their sexuality
D.      assumption that client problems are unrelated to social oppression or
stigma

64)     If included statistically as a form of elder abuse, self-neglect would      64. _____
represent about _____ percent of cases reported to state adult pro-
tective services agencies.

A.      5-10
B.      20-35
C.      40-50
D.      60-75

65)     Many social workers, especially those who work in institutional set-      65. _____
tings, use the brief treatment model in their interventions.  Which of the following is NOT one of the core assumptions of this model?

A.      Problems are a normal part of life and not a sign of pathology.
B.      Practitioners believe people can change, and communicate this to their
clients.
C.      The purpose of treatment is to develop insight into the underlying
causes of problems.
D.      Treatment makes use of what the client brings to it

66)     Stan, a Native American college student, is seeking information about      66. _____
work programs in the urban community where he lives.  When Stan asks a
female practitioner at the local agency about it, the practitioner notices that he
makes very little eye contact.  The practitioner should recognize that Stan

A.      would be more likely to look into her eyes if she were a male
B.      is not likely to follow through with the practitioner's recommendations
or referrals
C.      is likely to view direct eye contact as a lack of respect
D.      does not express much faith in the practitioner's abilities

67)    The tendency of people to perceive what they expect to perceive is a           67. _____
phenomenon known as

A.    self-serving bias
B.    perceptual set
C.    filtration
D.    fundamental attribution bias

68)    A person's satisfaction with communication is based upon a theoretical           68. _____
"sum total" of the positive and negative elements in a message.  This sum is a
phenomenon known as message

A.    validity
B.    salience
C.    solidity
D.    valence

69)    Data about how long or how often a problem occurs before an inter-           69. _____
vention are known as _____ data.

A.    raw
B.    norming
C.    baseline
D.    skewed

70)    In _____ social work, assessment is also known as           70. _____
functional analysis.

A.    narrative
B.    behavioral
C.    feminist
D.    cognitive

71)    During an assessment interview, a practitioner asks a client: "How do           71. _____
you feel about the fact that your drinking has harmed your relationship with
your daughter?"  The practitioner is trying to identify _____
consequences of the client's problem.

A.    contextual
B.    affective
C.    behavioral
D.    somatic

72)    For social work research to have a meaningful function, it must be ap-    72. _____
plied by practitioners.  One of the major reasons practitioners fail to apply the
results of research is that

A.    there is no standard methodology that would make results universally
applicable
B.    many studies lack relevance to day-to-day practice decisions
C.    there is still widespread theoretical bias in the design of many studies
D.    most practitioners don't conduct research themselves

73)    Of the following social sciences, social work draws most of its profes-    73. _____
sional expertise from

A.    psychology
B.    economics
C.    sociology
D.    anthropology

74)    In her meetings with a client, a practitioner has begun to form the per-    74. _____
ception that he may be using a combination of alcohol and illegal drugs.  She
decides, during subsequent meetings, to engage in "direct perception checking" in order to confirm or deny this perception.  This will involve

A.    paying careful attention to the client's tone of voice
B.    observing the client's behaviors to discover cues that will either con-
firm or deny her impressions
C.    asking the client if he has a drug or drinking problem
D.    listening more intently to the client's words and language

75)    Though practitioner self-disclosure can be a useful tool for helping    75. _____
clients, it is most helpful when its use is carefully assessed beforehand.  Generally, practitioners should AVOID making self-disclosure statements

A.    as concise as possible
B.    as a way of introducing oneself to the client
C.    in a way that will regulate the role distance between practitioner and
client
D.    similar in content and mood to the client's messages

# KEY (CORRECT ANSWERS)

| | | | | |
|---|---|---|---|---|
| 1. | A | | 41. | C |
| 2. | D | | 42. | A |
| 3. | C | | 43. | B |
| 4. | D | | 44. | D |
| 5. | B | | 45. | A |
| | | | | |
| 6. | D | | 46. | A |
| 7. | C | | 47. | C |
| 8. | B | | 48. | C |
| 9. | C | | 49. | A |
| 10. | D | | 50. | A |
| | | | | |
| 11. | D | | 51. | A |
| 12. | A | | 52. | D |
| 13. | B | | 53. | D |
| 14. | C | | 54. | D |
| 15. | B | | 55. | D |
| | | | | |
| 16. | D | | 56. | D |
| 17. | C | | 57. | A |
| 18. | B | | 58. | C |
| 19. | C | | 59. | C |
| 20. | B | | 60. | B |
| | | | | |
| 21. | D | | 61. | D |
| 22. | A | | 62. | A |
| 23. | D | | 63. | B |
| 24. | A | | 64. | C |
| 25. | B | | 65. | C |
| | | | | |
| 26. | B | | 66. | C |
| 27. | C | | 67. | B |
| 28. | A | | 68. | D |
| 29. | C | | 69. | C |
| 30. | C | | 70. | B |
| | | | | |
| 31. | A | | 71. | B |
| 32. | C | | 72. | B |
| 33. | A | | 73. | A |
| 34. | B | | 74. | B |
| 35. | B | | 75. | B |
| | | | | |
| 36. | C | | | |
| 37. | B | | | |
| 38. | B | | | |
| 39. | C | | | |
| 40. | C | | | |

# EXAMINATION SECTION
# TEST 1

DIRECTIONS: Each question or incomplete statement is followed by several suggested answers or completions. Select the one that BEST answers the question or completes the statement. *PRINT THE LETTER OF THE CORRECT ANSWER IN THE SPACE AT THE RIGHT.*

1. Recently, the State Department of Labor declared that *city employers are faced with a developing manpower shortage which will grow worse if business continues at high levels.* Since public welfare agencies have a special responsibility for preserving the self-maintenance capacities of physically handicapped persons, it is appropriate that during periods of increased employment such as that illustrated above, the Department of Welfare should place its GREATEST emphasis on    1.____

    A. developing special placement opportunities for all disabled persons
    B. providing vocational training for newly opened job opportunities
    C. recognizing that the disabled can never become as self-maintaining as the physically fit and will, therefore, continue to need assistance
    D. directing the disabled to those occupations related to the special senses which the disabled often develop
    E. facilitating the efforts of the disabled to obtain employment, whether temporary or permanent, partial or total

2. In order to meet more adequately the public assistance needs occasioned by sudden changes in the national economy, welfare agencies in general recommend, as a matter of preference, that    2.____

    A. each locality build up reserve funds to care for needy unemployed persons in order to avoid a breakdown of local resources such as occurred during the Depression
    B. the federal government assume total responsibility for the administration of public assistance
    C. state settlement laws be strictly enforced so that unemployed workers will be encouraged to move from the emergency industry centers to their former homes
    D. a federal-state-local program of general assistance be established with need as the only eligibility requirement
    E. eligibility requirements be tightened to assure that only legitimately worthy local residents receive the available assistance

3. The MOST practical method of maintaining income for the majority of aged persons who are no longer able to work, or for the families of those workers who are deceased, is    3.____

    A. a comprehensive system of non-categorical assistance on a basis of cash payments
    B. an integrated system of public assistance and extensive work relief programs
    C. a coordinated system of providing care in institutions and foster homes
    D. a system of contributory insurance in which a cash benefit is paid as a matter of right
    E. an expanded system of diagnostic and treatment centers

4. With the establishment of insurance and assistance programs under the Social Security Act, many institutional programs for the aged have tended to the greatest extent toward an increased emphasis on providing, of the following types of assistance,  4.____

    A. care for the aged by denominational groups
    B. care for children requiring institutional treatment
    C. recreational facilities for the able-bodied aged
    D. training facilities in industrial homework for the aged
    E. care for the chronically ill and infirm aged

5. According to studies made by the Federal Security Agency, the benefits received by beneficiaries of the old age and survivors insurance program during past years  5.____

    A. were too small to be basically helpful
    B. represented about a third of the resources of most beneficiaries
    C. were an unimportant factor in income maintenance
    D. constituted the major portion of the family's income
    E. constituted about one-quarter of the average public assistance grant

6. Of the following terms, the one which BEST describes the Social Security Act is  6.____

    A. enabling legislation    B. regulatory statute
    C. appropriations act    D. act of mandamus
    E. provisional enactment

7. Of the following, the term which MOST accurately describes an *appropriation* is  7.____

    A. authority to spend    B. itemized estimate
    C. *fund* accounting    D. anticipated expenditure
    E. executive budget

8. When business expansion causes a demand for labor, the worker group which benefits MOST immediately is the group comprising  8.____

    A. employed workers
    B. inexperienced workers under 21 years of age
    C. experienced workers 21 to 25 years of age
    D. inexperienced older workers
    E. experienced workers over 40 years of age

9. The MOST important failure in our present system of providing social work services in local communities is the  9.____

    A. absence of adequate facilities for treating mental illness
    B. lack of coordination of available data and service in the community
    C. poor quality of the casework services provided by the public agencies
    D. limitations of the probation and parole services
    E. inadequacy of private family welfare services

10. It is generally considered advisable for a public assistance agency to make special allowances for the purchase of physical appliances for its recipients only when the  10.____

    A. desired appliance has been prescribed by a physician and when the client is physically, mentally, and emotionally able to use it
    B. agency has a special fund to meet such additional expenditures

C. fact is verified that employment will be available if the client uses the appliance
D. purchase will assure the individual of becoming self-maintaining again
E. desired appliance has been prescribed by a social worker as necessary to compensate the client for loss of a normal bodily function

11. Recent studies of the relationship between incidence of illness and the use of available treatment services among various population groups in the United States show that        11.____

   A. while lower-income families use medical services with greater frequency, total expenditures are greater among the upper-income group
   B. although the average duration of a period of medical care increases with increasing income, the average frequency of obtaining care decreases with increasing income
   C. adequacy of medical service is inversely related to frequency of illness and size of family income
   D. families in the higher-income brackets have a heavier incidence of illness and make greater use of medical service than do those in the lower-income brackets
   E. both as to frequency and duration, the distribution of illness falls equally on all groups, but the use of medical service increases with income

12. The category of disease which most public health departments and authorities usually are NOT equipped to handle directly is that of        12.____

   A. chronic disease
   B. bronchial disturbances
   C. venereal disease
   D. mosquito-borne diseases
   E. incipient forms of tuberculosis

13. Recent statistical analyses of the causes of death in the United States indicate that medical science has now reached the stage where it would be preferable to increase its research toward control, among the following, PRINCIPALLY of        13.____

   A. accidents          B. suicides
   C. communicable diseases     D. chronic disease
   E. infant mortality

14. Although the distinction between mental disease and mental deficiency is fairly definite, both these conditions USUALLY represent        14.____

   A. diseases of one part or organ of the body rather than of the whole person
   B. an inadequacy existing from birth or shortly afterwards, and appearing as a simplicity of intelligence
   C. a deficiency developing later in life and characterized by distortions of attitude and belief
   D. inadequacies in meeting life situations and in conducting one's affairs
   E. somewhat transitory conditions characterized by disturbances of consciousness

15. According to studies made by reliable medical research organizations in the United States, differences among the states in proportion of physicians to population are MOST directly related to the        15.____

   A. geographic resources among the states
   B. skill of the physicians

C. relative proportions of urban and rural people in the population of the states
D. number of specialists in the ranks of the physicians
E. health status of the people in the various states

16. MOST of the mentally ill who are hospitalized for long periods of time are in institutions administered by    16.____

   A. the U.S. Public Health Service
   B. county and municipal government
   C. the Veterans Administration
   D. the state government
   E. psychiatrists in private practice

17. In the development and maintenance of a social group work program, it is accepted that certain principles must be recognized if the program is to achieve maximum value. Of the following, the one consideration which would be INAPPROPRIATE as a base on which to set the planning and operation of such a program is that it should    17.____

   A. be individualized and designed to meet specific needs
   B. develop out of interests and needs of group members
   C. be planned, conducted, and evaluated by the group
   D. involve the group worker as a helping person
   E. develop from a series of initial and follow-up surveys conducted by trained person-
      nel

18. One of the MAIN advantages of incorporating a charitable organization is that    18.____

   A. gifts or property of a corporation cannot be held in perpetuity
   B. gifts to unincorporated charitable organizations are not deductible from the taxable
      income
   C. incorporation gives less legal standing or *personality* than an informal partnership
   D. members of a corporation cannot be held liable for debts contracted by the organi-
      zation
   E. a corporate organization cannot be sued

19. In conjunction with court and educational authorities, the Division of Physically Handi-capped Children administers a program of care for persons under 2-1 years of age who, by reason of physical defect or infirmity, are totally or partially incapacitated for education or occupation. All of the following types of care are provided by this division EXCEPT    19.____

   A. surgical treatment
   B. medical treatment
   C. therapeutic treatment
   D. furnishing of prosthetic appliances or devices
   E. procuring scholarships for summer camps

20. If a client is to receive continuing services or assistance from the Department of Welfare requests help in which the Department has an interest and which it cannot provide, but which can be furnished by another agency in the community, the worker should USU-ALLY    20.____

A.  interpret the other agency's function to the client and determine how best to use its services, thus conserving the client's time and preventing possible embarrassment to him
B.  forego discussion of the other agency's services with the client, since it is confusing for two welfare agencies to attempt to serve the same client at the same time
C.  send a case summary to the other agency and request that a worker from that agency call at the client's home to assist in the working out of his problem
D.  not suggest the agency to which the client can apply and ask him to return and discuss the plans developed with the other agency
E.  not advise the client that his situation will be discussed with another agency in the community and that he will be notified whether the agency can accept his case and be of service to him

21. It is important to use a skilled worker to conduct the initial interview with an applicant for assistance in the Department of Welfare CHIEFLY because    21.____

A.  inaccurate information concerning eligibility requirements and the documentary evidence which must be produced may then be checked expeditiously
B.  whenever possible, the assistance plan should be developed during the course of the first interview
C.  only a highly skilled worker can make a satisfactory investigation of the applicant's eligibility
D.  the relationship established between worker and applicant during this interview usually determines the departmental policies affecting the case
E.  the effectiveness of the Department's subsequent work with the client is often influenced materially by the kind of relationship established in this first contact

22. During an interview, a client may seem overwhelmed by the amount of data needed by the Department of Welfare in order to establish his eligibility, although most of the required information, as a rule, is easily obtained.
The one of the following responses by the intake interviewer which could be expected to reassure such a client BEST is    22.____

A.  "All this information is very important and you should try your best to get it as soon as possible"
B.  "If you think you'll have trouble getting this material together, I'll do it for you"
C.  "It sounds like a lot, but it is actually very simple; without realizing it, you probably have most of the material on hand already"
D.  "There's no need to be overwhelmed by the amount of this material; all our clients have to get it together"
E.  "Oh, I'm sure you can do it"

23. Of the following objectives, the one which an initial interview with an applicant for public assistance is usually designed to serve is to    23.____

A.  afford the client an opportunity to express his needs and desires
B.  allow the worker time to secure all the information he wants
C.  condition the direction of service
D.  record verbatim the client's statement regarding need
E.  include a discussion of the client's family and other personal relationships

24. A MOST appropriate condition in the use of direct questions to obtain personal data in an interview is that, whenever possible,   24.____

    A. the direct questions be used only as a means of encouraging the person inter-viewed to talk about himself
    B. provision be made for recording the information
    C. the direct questions be used only after all other methods have failed
    D. the person being interviewed understand the reason for requesting the information
    E. the direct questions be used only at the start of the interview

25. Suppose that a social investigator, during his initial interview with a client, notices that the client is becoming antagonistic for no apparent reason.
In this situation, the investigator should USUALLY   25.____

    A. explain to the client that unwarranted antagonism is really due to factors deeply hidden in the client's own personality
    B. terminate the interview with a statement to the effect that the client should return for another interview when he feels more kindly disposed toward the interviewer
    C. make clear in his actions that there is no retaliatory disapproval and continue to try to understand the client's difficulties
    D. admit to the client that he is aware of the existing antagonism and that he is unable to find the reason for it
    E. ask the client why he feels antagonistic toward him since he himself has not given him any grounds for such a reaction

26. When a client informs the social investigator of a plan to move permanently to another state, it is the responsibility of the investigator to advise the client that   26.____

    A. he should apply for continued approval of his grant on the basis of *temporary absence* since his plan for permanent removal may not materialize
    B. the last check he receives before leaving the city should be used for necessary transportation and expenses while traveling to his new abode
    C. he will be ineligible for any continued assistance from the Department of Welfare and that eligibility in the new community will depend upon local requirements
    D. he should not move to a new state since the assistance in that state will probably not be adequate for his needs
    E. the Department of Welfare will arrange to have the public assistance agency in the community to which he is going make an immediate investigation in order that the continuance of his public assistance grant will not be interrupted

27. Suppose that the mother of a family receiving public assistance is recovering from an operation at home and that her doctor reports she will be unable to care for her children for one month.
In such a situation, it would be MOST appropriate for the social investigator to   27.____

    A. recommend the assignment of a Department of Welfare homemaker in accordance with the doctor's report
    B. refer the children to a temporary shelter
    C. visit the neighborhood to find a free home for the children
    D. recommend that foster care be provided
    E. write to legally responsible relatives living in an adjacent state to explore the possi-bility of their providing care for the children

28. In computing the budget for a family applying for public assistance where there is a lodger living in the household, Department of Welfare policy requires that the social investigator should deduct the                                                                              28.____

    A. total income received from the lodger from the total estimate of the family's needs
    B. total income from the lodger minus the cost of food for any meals provided from the total estimate of the family's needs
    C. total income from the lodger minus an adjusted allowance for fuel and lighting
    D. net income from the total estimate of the family's needs
    E. total income received from the lodger minus the proportionate cost of room rental

29. Experiences with respect to use of cash payments to public assistance clients have established that, basically, this form of assistance is more satisfactory than any other type because cash payments                                                                              29.____

    A. are less destructive of the client's self-respect than relief in kind
    B. are less likely to call for bookkeeping skill than payments by requisition
    C. are cheaper to administer than other forms of assistance
    D. are more acceptable to commercial concerns than order slips
    E. make possible larger grants to clients than other forms of assistance

Questions 30-39.

DIRECTIONS:   Levels of approval for certain types of allowances are set forth in the Department of Welfare manual, POLICIES GOVERNING THE ADMINISTRATION OF PUBLIC ASSISTANCE. In Questions 30 through 39 below are listed certain types of allowances for which approval is necessary according to departmental policy. Answer each of these questions in the following manner:

        ANSWER   IF THE TYPE OF ALLOWANCE REQUIRES APPROVAL OF
        A.      - the unit supervisor only
        B.      - the case supervisor in addition to the unit supervisor
        C.      - case consultation, in addition to unit and case supervisors
        D.      - case consultation and the resource division, in addition to unit and case supervisors
        E.      - the resource division, in addition to unit and case supervisors

30. Bond and mortgage waiver, after refusal to execute.                                                       30.____

31. Carfare to attend a special school for the blind and deaf.                                             31.____

32. Conditional sale and mortgage on personal property.                                                  32.____

33. Emergency assistance, first recurring or non-recurring agent.                                   33.____

34. Repair allowance for a homeowner.                                                                             34.____

35. Housing project security deposit.                                                                                35.____

36. Guide fees for blind persons.                                                                                       36.____

37. Rent arrears, including costs and fees.                                                                         37.____

38. Special diet, upon medical recommendation.                                                      38._____

39. Referral of a homeless man to a municipal shelter.                                               39._____

40. Coordination of staff activity in a large agency can usually be effected MOST success-          40._____
    fully by an executive through the use of

    A. written reports
    B. face-to-face contact in meetings with department heads
    C. observation of performance
    D. permanent assignment of staff to specific functions
    E. procedural instructions

41. Organization charts and manuals are essential to the sound administration of a public           41._____
    welfare agency.
    In this respect, the MOST important purpose of a manual in the Department of Welfare
    is to serve as a

    A. means of preventing duplication
    B. device for eliminating community misinterpretation of the Department's activities
    C. tool for achieving orderly operations
    D. method of maintaining executive controls
    E. system of compiling case decisions

42. Failure on the part of a caseworker in a public assistance agency to recognize the close        42._____
    relationship between standards of performance with regard to office routine and stan-
    dards of work with clients is, of the following, usually due to the fact that

    A. his supervisor has continued to assume responsibilities which the case worker
       should carry
    B. his supervisor has not made clear to the case worker each aspect of the job or of
       the total responsibilities of the worker
    C. the case worker should not be the person who is required to prepare reports
    D. the case worker's primary function is the treatment of social problems
    E. the clerical staff has not adequately performed those of its duties related to the
       work of the case worker

43. In helping a social investigator deal with a case in which the client is harassed by a diffi-    43._____
    cult family situation, the supervisor usually can be of GREATEST assistance by

    A. showing the investigator that his own family experiences parallel those of the client
    B. helping the investigator balance the interests of all members of the family
    C. advising the investigator that family matters are frequently too personal to be dis-
       cussed in detail
    D. suggesting that a psychiatrist be brought in on the case
    E. teaching the investigator how to discover which member of the family is most mal-
       adjusted

44. Initial interviews with applicants for public assistance require a high degree of skill on the part of the interviewer PRIMARILY because

    44.____

  A. applicants are usually uncertain as to what kind of factual information will aid their cause
  B. applicants who have had no previous experience with social agencies usually are overwhelmed by the newness of the experience
  C. the feeling of economic dependency is usually emotionally disturbing to the applicant
  D. applicants are naturally suspicious of any agency that administers public funds
  E. the worker and the applicant are strangers to one another and each is uncertain as to how the other will interpret his remarks

45. During a case conference, if a unit supervisor repeatedly returns to a statement of points already made, the case supervisor should USUALLY

    45.____

  A. discuss some neutral subject until the unit supervisor is more composed
  B. insert a question leading to a different topic altogether
  C. terminate the conference as soon as possible in order not to waste time
  D. attempt to direct the flow of discussion by expressing his own opinion on the subject
  E. let the unit supervisor talk himself out on this topic

46. With respect to case recording, the Department of Welfare has developed a new type of streamlined case record which will contain all the essential factors pertinent to current eligibility and which can be maintained in a usable and readable condition on a continuing basis. The development of this plan was based on a consideration of the essential attributes of good recording in a public assistance agency. Of the following, the one which is NOT in accord with the above-mentioned plan is

    46.____

  A. accuracy in recording, which reflects the point of view of the client and of the social investigator
  B. elimination of all information except the documentation of eligibility based on points of statutory evidence
  C. freedom from bias or prejudice in order that the client may receive the full service due to him
  D. brevity and conciseness, which make the record more serviceable for review by the social investigator and by his supervisors
  E. clarity, which is obtained largely by adherence to common rules of rhetoric and which provides coherence and unity

47. When Children's Placement Services refers an undercare case to a welfare center for public assistance, the social investigator to whom the case is assigned should

    47.____

  A. review the investigation made by Children's Placement Services and supplement it with whatever information is necessary
  B. accept the case as referred for the appropriate type of public assistance
  C. make a complete investigation of all factors of eligibility in the same manner as for any other applicant for public assistance
  D. talk to the client and make a referral to a private agency
  E. make an immediate referral of the client to an available job in order to prevent dependency

48. Under certain circumstances, a court order imposes responsibility on the unmarried mother and the father for sharing the support of a child born out of wedlock. The court which has jurisdiction over such matters is the

    A. Supreme Court
    C. Magistrates' Court
    E. Court of Special Sessions
    B. Children's Court
    D. Domestic Relations Court

48.____

49. Social workers who work principally with maladjusted children find that the children's problems MOST frequently originate in

    A. health factors
    C. teachers' attitudes
    E. economic conditions
    B. religious attitudes
    D. parental attitudes

49.____

50. Persistent feeding difficulties in children are MOST often related to

    A. poverty in the home
    B. basic personality maladjustments
    C. high intelligence
    D. the presence of other children in the room
    E. the number of older and younger children in the family

50.____

51. If a person attempts to conceal his inadequacies in certain activities by overindulging in some other activity, he is MOST liable to do so because he

    A. is compensating for his inadequacies
    B. has a delusion that he is inadequate in some activities
    C. has rationalized that the skill in the latter activity is more easily developed
    D. is trying to develop skill in the former activities by indulging in the latter
    E. is projecting the pleasure he finds in the former activities to the latter

51.____

52. The casework concept of *acceptable*, when applied to behavior that deviates from what society expects, implies

    A. refusing to pass judgment on the behavior of others
    B. accepting all behavior without attempting to evaluate it
    C. condoning behavior which the client seems incapable of changing
    D. exercising non-judgmental impartiality
    E. active understanding of the underlying feelings rather than of the behavior itself

52.____

53. When a prospective employer requests that a person of a particular race, color, or religion be sent to him in order to fill a job opening in a department store, the employment interviewer should IMMEDIATELY

    A. report the employer to the State Commission Against Discrimination
    B. advise the employer that he is violating the law and that if he does not accept an able and available person, he will be reported to the State Commission Against Discrimination
    C. remove the employer's name as a source of employment referrals and notify Central Office so that other welfare centers may be informed of the situation
    D. arrange to interview the employer in order to determine whether there are valid reasons for his request
    E. make an employment referral if a public assistance recipient who meets the specifications of the employer is available

53.____

54. The early English Poor Laws influenced American administration of relief in their empha-   54.____
sis upon the

    A. giving of adequate assistance
    B. centralization of relief administration under a national authority
    C. local character of administration and financing
    D. failure to enforce the responsibility of relatives for their needy kin
    E. discrimination made in providing for the care and treatment of clients on the basis
       of their individual needs

55. The undifferentiated treatment of clients given by public welfare services in the eigh-   55.____
teenth and nineteenth centuries was due not only to the state of social and economic
development but also to the

    A. limitations imposed by the lack of adequate institutional facilities
    B. prevalence of religious condemnation of social inadequacy
    C. absence of technical knowledge necessary for social diagnosis
    D. homogeneous nature of the social structure itself
    E. relative isolation of individual communities

---

# KEY (CORRECT ANSWERS)

| | | | | | | | |
|---|---|---|---|---|---|---|---|
| 1. | E | 16. | D | 31. | A | 46. | B |
| 2. | D | 17. | E | 32. | C | 47. | A |
| 3. | D | 18. | D | 33. | A | 48. | E |
| 4. | E | 19. | E | 34. | E | 49. | D |
| 5. | D | 20. | A | 35. | A | 50. | B |
| 6. | A | 21. | E | 36. | B | 51. | A |
| 7. | A | 22. | C | 37. | B | 52. | D |
| 8. | B | 23. | A | 38. | A | 53. | B |
| 9. | B | 24. | D | 39. | A | 54. | C |
| 10. | A | 25. | C | 40. | B | 55. | C |
| 11. | C | 26. | C | 41. | C | | |
| 12. | A | 27. | A | 42. | B | | |
| 13. | D | 28. | A | 43. | B | | |
| 14. | D | 29. | A | 44. | C | | |
| 15. | C | 30. | D | 45. | B | | |

---

# EXAMINATION SECTION
# TEST 1

DIRECTIONS: Each question or incomplete statement is followed by several suggested answers or completions. Select the one that BEST answers the question or completes the statement. *PRINT THE LETTER OF THE CORRECT ANSWER IN THE SPACE AT THE RIGHT.*

1. Assume that you are a supervisor. One of the workers under your supervision is careless about the routine aspects of his work.
   Of the following, the action MOST likely to develop in this worker a better attitude toward job routines is to demonstrate that

   A. it is just as easy to do his job the right way
   B. organization of his job will leave more time for field work
   C. the routine part of the job is essential to performing a good piece of work
   D. job routines are a responsibility of the worker

   1.____

2. A supervisor can MOST effectively secure necessary improvement in a worker's office work by

   A. encouraging the worker to keep abreast of his work
   B. relating the routine part of his job to the total job to be done
   C. helping the worker to establish a good system for covering his office work and holding him to it
   D. informing the worker that he will be required to organize his work more efficiently

   2.____

3. A supervisor should offer criticism in such a manner that the criticism is helpful and not overwhelming.
   Of the following, the LEAST valid inference that can be drawn on the basis of the above statement is that a supervisor should

   A. demonstrate that the criticism is partial and not total
   B. give criticism in such a way that it does not undermine the worker's self-confidence
   C. keep his relationships with the worker objective
   D. keep criticism directed towards general work performance

   3.____

4. The one of the following areas in which a worker may LEAST reasonably expect direct assistance from the supervisor is in

   A. building up rapport with all clients
   B. gaining insight into the unmet needs of clients
   C. developing an understanding of community resources
   D. interpreting agency policies and procedures

   4.____

5. You are informed that a worker under your supervision has submitted a letter complaining of an unfair service rating. Of the following, the MOST valid assumption for you to make concerning this worker is that he should be

   A. more adequately supervised in the future
   B. called in for a supervisory conference
   C. given a transfer to some other unit where he may be more happy
   D. given no more consideration than any other inefficient worker

   5.____

6. Assume that you are a supervisor. You find that a somewhat bewildered worker, newly    6.____
appointed to the department, hesitates to ask questions for fear of showing his ignorance
and jeopardizing his position.
Of the following, the BEST procedure for you to follow is to

    A.  try to discover the reason for his evident fear of authority
    B.  tell him that when he is in doubt about a procedure or a policy, he should consult
        his fellow workers
    C.  develop with the worker a plan for more frequent supervisory conferences
    D.  explain why each staff member is eager to give him any available information that
        will help him do a good job

7. Of the following, the MOST effective method of helping a newly appointed worker adjust    7.____
to his new job is to

    A.  assure him that with experience his uncertain attitudes will be replaced by a pro-
        fessional approach
    B.  help him, by accepting him as he is, to have confidence in his ability to handle the
        job
    C.  help him to be on guard against the development of punitive attitudes
    D.  help him to recognize the mutability of the agency's policies and procedures

8. Suppose that, as a supervisor, you have scheduled an individual conference with an    8.____
experienced worker under your supervision.
Of the following, the BEST plan of action for this conference is to

    A.  discuss the cases that the worker is most interested in
    B.  plan with the worker to cover the problems in his cases that are difficult for him
    C.  advise the worker that the conference is his to do with as he sees fit
    D.  spot check the worker's case load in advance and select those cases for discus-
        sion in which the worker has done poor work

9. Of the following, the CHIEF function of a supervisor should be to    9.____

    A.  assist in the planning of new policies and the evaluation of existing ones
    B.  promote congenial relationships among members of the staff
    C.  achieve optimum functioning of each unit and each worker
    D.  promote the smooth functioning of job routines

10. The competent supervisor must realize the importance of planning.    10.____
Of the following, the aspect of planning which is LEAST appropriately considered a
responsibility of the supervisor is

    A.  long-range planning for the proper functioning of his unit
    B.  planning to take care of peak and slack periods
    C.  planning to cover agency policies in group conferences
    D.  long-range planning to develop community resources

11. The one of the following objectives which should be of LEAST concern to the supervisor    11._____
in the performance of his duties is to

    A.  help the worker to make friends with all of his clients
    B.  be impartial and fair to all members of the staff
    C.  stimulate the worker's growth on the job
    D.  meet the needs of individual workers for case work guidance

12. The one of the following which is LEAST properly considered a direct responsibility of the    12._____
supervisor is

    A.  liaison between the staff and the administrator
    B.  interpreting administrative orders and procedures to the worker
    C.  training new workers
    D.  maintaining staff morale at a high level

13. In order to teach the worker to develop an objective approach, the BEST action for the    13._____
supervisor to take is to help the worker to

    A.  develop a sincere interest in his job
    B.  understand the varied responsibilities that are an integral part of his job
    C.  differentiate clearly between himself as a friend and as a case worker
    D.  find satisfaction in his work

14. If the worker shows excessive submission which indicates a need for dependence on the    14._____
supervisor in handling a case, it would be MOST advisable for the supervisor to

    A.  indicate firmly that the worker-supervisor relationship does not call for submission
    B.  define areas of responsibility of worker and of supervisor
    C.  recognize the worker's need to be sustained and supported and help him by mak-
ing decisions for him
    D.  encourage the worker to do his best to overcome his handicap

15. Assume that, as a supervisor, you are conducting a group conference.    15._____
Of the following, the BEST procedure for you to follow in order to stimulate group discussion is to

    A.  permit the active participation of all members
    B.  direct the discussion to an acceptable conclusion
    C.  resolve conflicts of opinion among members of the group
    D.  present a question for discussion on which the group members have some knowl-
edge or experience

16. Suppose that, as a new supervisor, you wish to inform the staff under your supervision of    16._____
your methods of operation. Of the following, the BEST procedure for you to follow is to

    A.  advise the staff that they will learn gradually from experience
    B.  inform each worker in an individual conference
    C.  call a group conference for this purpose
    D.  distribute a written memorandum among all members of the staff

17. The MOST constructive and effective method of correcting a worker who has made a mistake is, in general, to    17.____

    A. explain that his evaluation is related to his errors
    B. point out immediately where he erred and tell him how it should have been done
    C. show him how to readjust his methods so as to avoid similar errors in the future
    D. try to discover by an indirect method why the error was made

18. The MOST effective method for the supervisor to follow in order to obtain the cooperation of a worker under his supervision is, wherever possible, to    18.____

    A. maintain a careful record of performance in order to keep the worker on his toes
    B. give the worker recognition in order to promote greater effort and give him more satisfaction in his work
    C. try to gain the worker's cooperation for the good of the welfare service
    D. advise the worker that his advancement on the job depends on his cooperation

19. Of the following, the MOST appropriate initial course for a worker to take when he is unable to clarify a policy with his supervisor is to    19.____

    A. bring up the problem at the next group conference
    B. discuss the policy immediately with his fellow workers
    C. accept the supervisor's interpretation as final
    D. determine what responsibility he has for putting the policy into effect

20. Good administration allows for different treatment of different workers. Of the following, the CHIEF implication of this statement is that    20.____

    A. it would be unfair for the supervisor not to treat all staff members alike
    B. fear of favoritism tends to undermine staff morale
    C. best results are obtained by individualization within the limits of fair treatment
    D. difficult problems call for a different kind of approach

21. The MOST effective and appropriate method of building efficiency and morale in a group of workers is, in general,    21.____

    A. by stressing the economic motive
    B. through use of the authority inherent in the position
    C. by a friendly approach to all
    D. by a discipline that is fair but strict

22. Of the following, the LEAST valid basis for the assignment of work to an employee is the    22.____

    A. kind of service to be rendered
    B. experience and training of the worker
    C. health and capacity of the worker
    D. racial composition of the community where the office is located

23. The CHIEF justification for staff education, consisting of in-service training, lies in its con-    23.____
tribution to

    A. improvement in the quality of work performed
    B. recruitment of a better type of worker to the department
    C. employee morale, accruing from a feeling of growth on the job
    D. the satisfaction that the worker gets on his job

24. Suppose that you are a supervisor. A worker no longer with the department requests    24.____
you, as his former supervisor, to write a letter recommending him for a position with a private organization.
Of the following, the BEST procedure for you to follow is to include in the letter only
information that

    A. will help the applicant get the job
    B. is clear, factual, and substantiated
    C. is known to you personally
    D. can readily be corroborated by personal interview

25. Of the following, the MOST important item on which to base the efficiency evaluation of a    25.____
worker under your supervision is

    A. the nature of the relationship that he has built up with his clients
    B. how he gets along with his fellow employees
    C. his personal habits and skills
    D. the effectiveness of his control over his case load

# KEY (CORRECT ANSWERS)

| 1. D | 11. A |
|------|-------|
| 2. B | 12. A |
| 3. D | 13. C |
| 4. A | 14. B |
| 5. B | 15. D |
| 6. C | 16. C |
| 7. B | 17. C |
| 8. B | 18. B |
| 9. C | 19. D |
| 10. D | 20. C |

21. D
22. D
23. A
24. B
25. D

# TEST 2

DIRECTIONS: Each question or incomplete statement is followed by several suggested answers or completions. Select the one that BEST answers the question or completes the statement. *PRINT THE LETTER OF THE CORRECT ANSWER IN THE SPACE AT THE RIGHT*

1. According to generally accepted personnel practice, the MOST effective method of building morale in a new worker is to    1.____

   A. exercise caution in praising the worker, lest he become overconfident
   B. give sincere and frank commendation whenever possible in order to stimulate interest and effort
   C. praise the worker highly even for mediocre performance so that he will be stimulated to do better
   D. warn the worker frequently that he cannot hope to succeed unless he puts forth his best effort

2. Errors made by newly appointed workers often follow a predictable pattern. The one of the following errors likely to have LEAST serious consequences is the tendency of a new worker to    2.____

   A. discuss problems that are outside his province with the client
   B. persuade the client to accept the worker's solution of a problem
   C. be too strict in carrying out departmental policy and procedure
   D. depend upon the use of authority due to his inexperience and lack of skill in working with people

3. Of the following, the BEST method of helping the new worker to apply social case work principles is, in general, through    3.____

   A. the medium of the individual conference
   B. reading generally accepted authorities on the subject
   C. the medium of his own cases
   D. a course of study for him to follow

4. The MOST effective way for a supervisor to break down a worker's defensive stand against supervisory guidance is to    4.____

   A. come to an understanding with him on the mutual responsibilities involved in the job of the worker and supervisor
   B. tell him he must feel free to express his opinions and to discuss basic problems
   C. show him how to develop toward greater objectivity, sensitivity, and understanding
   D. advise him that it is necessary to carry out agency policy and procedures in order to do a good job

5. Of the following, the LEAST essential function of the supervisor who is conducting a group conference should be to    5.____

   A. keep attention focused on the purpose of the conference
   B. encourage discussion of controversial points
   C. make certain that all possible viewpoints are discussed
   D. be thoroughly prepared in advance

6. When conducting a group conference, the supervisor should be LEAST concerned with    6.\_\_\_\_

    A. providing an opportunity for the free interchange of ideas
    B. imparting knowledge and understanding of case work
    C. leading the discussion toward a planned goal
    D. pointing out where individual workers have erred in case work practice

7. If the participants in a conference are unable to agree on the proper application of a concept to the work of the department, the MOST suitable temporary procedure for the supervisor to follow is to    7.\_\_\_\_

    A. suggest that each member think the subject through before the next meeting
    B. tell the group to examine their differences for possible conflicts with present policies
    C. suggest that practices can be changed because of new conditions
    D. state the acceptable practice in the agency and whether deviations from such practice can be permitted

8. If a worker is to participate constructively in any group discussion, it is MOST important that he have    8.\_\_\_\_

    A. advance notice of the agenda for the meeting
    B. long experience in the department
    C. knowledge and experience in social work
    D. the ability to assume a leadership role

9. Of the following, the MOST important principle for the supervisor to follow when conducting a group discussion is that he should    9.\_\_\_\_

    A. move the discussion toward acceptance by the group of a particular point of view
    B. express his ideas clearly and succinctly
    C. lead the group to accept the authority inherent in his position
    D. contribute to the discussion from his knowledge and experience

10. The one of the following which is considered LEAST important as a purpose of the group conference is to    10.\_\_\_\_

    A. provide for a free exchange of ideas among the members of the group
    B. evaluate case work methods and procedures in order to protect the members from individual criticism
    C. provide an opportunity to interpret procedures and general case work practices
    D. pool the experience of the group members for the benefit of all

11. In order for the evaluation conference to stimulate MOST effectively the worker's professional growth on the job, it should    11.\_\_\_\_

    A. start him thinking about his present status with the agency
    B. show him the necessity for taking stock of his total performance
    C. give him a sense of direction in relation to his future development
    D. give him a better perspective on the work of the department

12. The PRIMARY consideration in good case recording is that the case history should          12._____

    A. be written simply and contain only significant and relevant material
    B. contain subjective material needed on the case
    C. be written concisely and clearly in good English
    D. include points of interest to both the worker and the supervisor

13. Of the following, the MOST important purpose of the case record summary in the depart-          13._____
ment of welfare is to

    A. acquaint the worker with forgotten details of the case
    B. provide a review of the client's status and eligibility
    C. provide a detailed picture of what has happened in the case
    D. give the worker a new perspective on the case

14. The development of good public relations in the area for which the supervisor is respon-          14._____
sible should be considered by the supervisor as

    A. not his responsibility as he is primarily responsible for his workers' services
    B. dependent upon him as he is in the best position to interpret the department to the
community
    C. not important to the adequate functioning of the department
    D. a part of his method of carrying out his job responsibility as what his workers do
affect the community

15. Assume that you are a supervisor. A newly appointed worker under your supervision          15._____
asks you what action he should take when, finding it necessary to refuse relief to a client,
the client becomes unusually belligerent and refuses to listen to reason.
Of the following, the BEST advice for you to give the worker is to

    A. refer the client to the case supervisor
    B. explain to the client at length the reasons for the refusal
    C. carefully explore with the client all possible courses of action
    D. be firm and definite in his refusal

16. Of the following, the LEAST accurate statement concerning the relationship of public and          16._____
private social agencies is that

    A. both have an important and necessary function to perform
    B. they are not to be considered as competing or rival agencies
    C. they are cooperating agencies
    D. their work is based on fundamentally different social work concepts

17. Of the following, the LEAST accurate statement concerning the worker-client relationship          17._____
is that the worker should have the ability to

    A. express warmth of feeling in appropriate ways as a basis for a professional rela-
tionship which creates confidence
    B. feel appropriately in the relationship without losing the ability to see the situation in
the perspective necessary to help the people immersed in it
    C. identify himself with the client so that the worker's personality does not influence
the client
    D. use keen observation and perceive what is significant with a new range of appreci-
ation of the meaning of the situation to the client

18. Of the following, the MOST fundamental psychological concept underlying case work in     18._____
the public assistance field is that

    A. eligibility for public assistance should be reviewed from time to time
    B. workers should be aware of the prevalence of psychological disabilities among members of families on public assistance
    C. workers should realize the necessity of carrying out the policies laid down by the state office in order that state aid may be received
    D. in the process of receiving assistance, recipients should not be deprived of their normal status of self-direction

19. Of the following, the MOST comprehensive, as well as the MOST accurate, statement     19._____
concerning the professional attitude of the social worker is that he should

    A. have a real concern for, and an intelligent interest in, the welfare of the client
    B. recognize that the client's feelings rather than the realities of his needs are of major importance to the client
    C. put at the client's service the worker's knowledge and sincere interest in him
    D. use his insight and understanding to make sound decisions about the client

20. The one of the following reasons for refusing a job which is LEAST acceptable, from the     20._____
viewpoint of maintaining a client's continued rights to unemployment insurance benefits,
is that

    A. acceptance of the job would interfere with the client's joining or retaining membership in a labor union
    B. there is a strike, lockout, or other industrial controversy in the establishment where employment is offered
    C. the distance from the place of employment to his home is greater than seems justified to the client
    D. the wages offered are lower than the prevailing wages in that locality

21. The one of the following statements concerning the division of veterans assistance which     21._____
is LEAST accurate is that the service includes

    A. the arrangement of occupational registration, vocational rehabilitation, and employment referrals for veterans and their dependents
    B. aid in obtaining citizenship papers under special naturalization, laws applicable only to veterans
    C. the handling of claims for burial expenses of deceased honorably discharged veterans
    D. providing for hospital care and domiciliary care at soldiers' homes

22. Whenever possible, a client on home relief who is eligible for assistance under one of the three categories should be changed to categorical relief.
Of the following, the LEAST accurate statement regarding this change is that    22.____

   A. change to categorical relief increases public understanding of the purposes and functioning of relief
   B. change to categorical relief is in accordance with the plan of the state department of welfare
   C. the Federal government reimburses the state and city for a percentage under the categories
   D. the welfare client will be better served under one of the forms of categorical relief

23. The LEAST accurate of the following statements regarding the functions of the transportation unit of the department of welfare is that it    23.____

   A. provides transportation for persons who have verified offers of employment in states which border on New York State
   B. determines eligibility for payment of transportation expenses
   C. makes reservations and purchases tickets for blind clients who are leaving for temporary periods
   D. is authorized to furnish transportation to all those who meet requirements regardless of whether or not they are in receipt of public assistance

24. The PRIMARY purpose of the welfare department will be BEST fulfilled, insofar as the giving of public assistance is concerned, if the rules and regulations are interpreted    24.____

   A. to the end that the most economical operation of the department will result
   B. strictly according to written instructions
   C. with special consideration for those applicants having the greatest needs
   D. insofar as possible in line with each applicant's circumstances and needs

25. The National Mental Health Act provides for    25.____

   A. an appropriation of five million dollars for research on mental illness
   B. the organization of a National Mental Health Institution within the structure of the Public Health Service
   C. an appropriation of five million dollars for grants-in-aid to the states for research and expansion of training and clinical facilities
   D. the establishment of Mental Hygiene Clinics in certain specified areas

## KEY (CORRECT ANSWERS)

| 1. B | 6. D | 11. C | 16. D | 21. D |
|------|------|-------|-------|-------|
| 2. C | 7. D | 12. A | 17. C | 22. D |
| 3. C | 8. A | 13. B | 18. D | 23. A |
| 4. A | 9. D | 14. D | 19. C | 24. D |
| 5. B | 10. B | 15. D | 20. C | 25. B |

# INTERVIEWING
## EXAMINATION SECTION
## TEST 1

DIRECTIONS: Each question or incomplete statement is followed by several suggested answers or completions. Select the one that BEST answers the question or completes the statement. *PRINT THE LETTER OF THE CORRECT ANSWER IN THE SPACE AT THE RIGHT.*

1. An interview is BEST conducted in private primarily because

    A. the person interviewed will tend to be less self-conscious
    B. the interviewer will be able to maintain his continuity of thought better
    C. it will insure that the interview is "off the record"
    D. people tend to "show off" before an audience

1.\_\_\_\_

2. An interviewer can BEST establish a good relationship with the person being interviewed by

    A. assuming casual interest in the statements made by the person being interviewed
    B. taking the point of view of the person interviewed
    C. controlling the interview to a major extent
    D. showing a genuine interest in the person

2.\_\_\_\_

3. An interviewer will be better able to understand the person interviewed and his problems if he recognizes that much of the person's behavior is due to motives

    A. which are deliberate
    B. of which he is unaware
    C. which are inexplicable
    D. which are kept under control

3.\_\_\_\_

4. An interviewer's attention must be directed toward himself as well as toward the person interviewed. This statement means that the interviewer should

    A. keep in mind the extent to which his own prejudices may influence his judgment
    B. rationalize the statements made by the person interviewed
    C. gain the respect and confidence of the person interviewed
    D. avoid being too impersonal

4.\_\_\_\_

5. More complete expression will be obtained from a person being interviewed if the interviewer can create the impression that

    A. the data secured will become part of a permanent record
    B. official information must be accurate in every detail
    C. it is the duty of the person interviewed to give accurate data
    D. the person interviewed is participating in a discussion of his own problems

5.\_\_\_\_

6. The practice of asking leading questions should be avoided in an interview because the

    A. interviewer risks revealing his attitudes to the person being interviewed
    B. interviewer may be led to ignore the objective attitudes of the person interviewed
    C. answers may be unwarrantedly influenced
    D. person interviewed will resent the attempt to lead him and will be less cooperative

6.\_\_\_\_

7. A good technique for the interviewer to use in an effort to secure reliable data and to    7.\_\_\_\_
reduce the possibility of misunderstanding is to

    A. use casual undirected conversation, enabling the person being interviewed to talk about himself, and thus secure the desired information
    B. adopt the procedure of using direct questions regularly
    C. extract the desired information from the person being interviewed by putting him on the defensive
    D. explain to the person being interviewed the information desired and the reason for needing it

8. You are interviewing a patient to determine whether she is eligible for medical assis-    8.\_\_\_\_
tance. Of the many questions that you have to ask her, some are routine questions that patients tend to answer willingly and easily. Other questions are more personal and some patients tend to resent being asked them and avoid answering them directly. For you to begin the interview with the more personal questions would be

    A. *desirable,* because the end of the interview will go smoothly and the patient will be left with a warm feeling
    B. *undesirable,* because the patient might not know the answers to the questions
    C. *desirable,* because you will be able to return to these questions later to verify the accuracy of the responses
    D. *undesirable,* because you might antagonize the patient before you have had a chance to establish rapport

9. While interviewing a patient about her family composition, the patient asks you whether    9.\_\_\_\_
you are married.
Of the following, the MOST appropriate way for you to handle this situation is to

    A. answer the question briefly and redirect her back to the topic under discussion
    B. refrain from answering the question and proceed with the interview
    C. advise the patient that it is more important that she answer your questions than that you answer hers, and proceed with the interview
    D. promise the patient that you will answer her question later, in the hope that she will forget, and redirect her back to the topic under discussion

10. In response to a question about his employment history, a patient you are interviewing    10.\_\_\_\_
rambles and talks about unrelated matters.
Of the following, the MOST appropriate course of action for you to take FIRST is to

    A. ask questions to direct the patient back to his employment history
    B. advise him to concentrate on your questions and not to discuss irrelevant information
    C. ask him why he is resisting a discussion of his employment history
    D. advise him that if you cannot get the information you need, he will not be eligible for medical assistance

11. Suppose that a person you are interviewing becomes angry at some of the questions     11.____
you have asked, calls you meddlesome and nosy, and states that she will not answer
those questions.
Of the following, which is the BEST action for you to take?

    A. Explain the reasons the questions are asked and the importance of the answers.
    B. Inform the interviewee that you are only doing your job and advise her that she
       should answer your questions or leave the office.
    C. Report to your supervisor what the interviewee called you and refuse to continue
       the interview.
    D. End the interview and tell the interviewee she will not be serviced by your depart-
       ment.

12. Suppose that during the course of an interview the interviewee demands in a very rude     12.____
way that she be permitted to talk to your supervisor or someone in charge.
Which of the following is probably the BEST way to handle this situation?

    A. Inform your supervisor of the demand and ask her to speak to the interviewee.
    B. Pay no attention to the demands of the interviewee and continue the interview.
    C. Report to your supervisor and tell her to get another interviewer for this inter-
       viewee.
    D. Tell her you are the one "in charge" and that she should talk to you.

13. Of the following, the outcome of an interview by an aide depends MOST heavily on the     13.____

    A. personality of the interviewee
    B. personality of the aide
    C. subject matter of the questions asked
    D. interaction between aide and interviewee

14. Some patients being interviewed are primarily interested in making a favorable impres-     14.____
sion. The aide should be aware of the fact that such patients are more likely than other
patients to

    A. try to anticipate the answers the interviewer is looking for
    B. answer all questions openly and frankly
    C. try to assume the role of interviewer
    D. be anxious to get the interview over as quickly as possible

15. The type of interview which an aide usually conducts is substantially different from most     15.____
interviewing situations in all of the following aspects EXCEPT the

    A. setting                  B. kinds of clients
    C. techniques employed     D. kinds of problems

16. During an interview, an aide uses a "leading question." This type of question is so-called     16.____
because it generally

    A. starts a series of questions about one topic
    B. suggests the answer which the aide wants
    C. forms the basis for a following "trick" question
    D. sets, at the beginning, the tone of the interview

17. Casework interviewing is always directed to the client and his situation. The one of the following which is the MOST accurate statement with respect to the proper focus of an interview is that the 17._____

    A. caseworker limits the client to concentration on objective data
    B. client is generally permitted to talk about facts and feelings with no direction from the caseworker
    C. main focus in casework interviews is on feelings rather than facts
    D. caseworker is responsible for helping the client focus on any material which seems to be related to his problems or difficulties

18. Assume that you are conducting a training program for the caseworkers under your supervision. At one of the sessions, you discuss the problem of interviewing a dull and stupid client who gives a slow and disconnected case history. The BEST of the following interviewing methods for you to recommend in such a case in order to ascertain the facts is for the caseworker to 18._____

    A. ask the client leading questions requiring "yes" or "no" answers
    B. request the client to limit his narration to the essential facts so that the interview can be kept as brief as possible
    C. review the story with the client, patiently asking simple questions
    D. tell the client that unless he is more cooperative he cannot be helped to solve his problem

19. A recent development in casework interviewing procedure, known as multiple-client interviewing, consists of interviews of the entire family at the same time. However, this may not be an effective casework method in certain situations. Of the following, the situation in which the standard individual interview would be preferable is when 19._____

    A. family members derive consistent and major gratification from assisting each other in their destructive responses
    B. there is a crucial family conflict to which the members are reacting
    C. the family is overwhelmed by interpersonal anxieties which have not been explored
    D. the worker wants to determine the pattern of family interaction to further his diagnostic understanding

20. A follow-up interview was arranged for an applicant in order that he could furnish certain requested evidence. At this follow-up interview, the applicant still fails to furnish the necessary evidence. It would be MOST advisable for you to 20._____

    A. advise the applicant that he is now considered ineligible
    B. ask the applicant how soon he can get the necessary evidence and set a date for another interview
    C. question the applicant carefully and thoroughly to determine if he has misrepresented or falsified any information
    D. set a date for another interview and tell the applicant to get the necessary evidence by that time.

# KEY (CORRECT ANSWERS)

| | | | | |
|---|---|---|---|---|
| 1. | A | | 11. | A |
| 2. | D | | 12. | A |
| 3. | B | | 13. | D |
| 4. | A | | 14. | A |
| 5. | D | | 15. | C |
| 6. | C | | 16. | B |
| 7. | D | | 17. | D |
| 8. | D | | 18. | C |
| 9. | A | | 19. | A |
| 10. | A | | 20. | B |

———

# TEST 2

DIRECTIONS: Each question or incomplete statement is followed by several suggested answers or completions. Select the one that BEST answers the question or completes the statement. *PRINT THE LETTER OF THE CORRECT ANSWER IN THE SPACE AT THE RIGHT.*

1. In interviewing, the practice of anticipating an applicant's answers to questions is generally          1._____

   A. *desirable,* because it is effective and economical when it is necessary to interview large numbers of applicants
   B. *desirable,* because many applicants have language difficulties
   C. *undesirable,* because it is the inalienable right of every person to answer as he sees fit
   D. *undesirable,* because applicants may tend to agree with the answer proposed by the interviewer even when the answer is not entirely correct

2. When an initial interview is being conducted, one way of starting is to explain the purpose of the interview to the applicant. The practice of starting the interview with such an explanation is generally          2._____

   A. *desirable,* because the applicant can then understand why the interview is necessary and what will be accomplished by it
   B. *desirable,* because it creates the rapport which is necessary to successful interviewing
   C. *undesirable,* because time will be saved by starting directly with the questions which must be asked
   D. *undesirable,* because the interviewer should have the choice of starting an interview in any manner he prefers

3. For you to use responses such as "That's interesting," "Uh-huh" and "Good" during an interview with a patient is          3._____

   A. *desirable,* because they indicate that the investigator is attentive
   B. *undesirable,* because they are meaningless to the patient
   C. *desirable,* because the investigator is not supposed to talk excessively
   D. *undesirable,* because they tend to encourage the patient to speak freely

4. During the course of a routine interview, the BEST tone of voice for an interviewer to use is          4._____

   A. authoritative               B. uncertain
   C. formal                      D. conversational

5. It is recommended that interviews which inquire into the personal background of an individual should be held in private. The BEST reason for this practice is that privacy          5._____

   A. allows the individual to talk freely about the details of his background
   B. induces contemplative thought on the part of the interviewed individual
   C. prevents any interruptions by departmental personnel during the interview
   D. most closely resembles the atmosphere of the individual's personal life

6. Assume that you are interviewing a patient to determine whether he has any savings accounts. To obtain this information, the MOST effective way to phrase your question would be:

    A. "You don't have any savings, do you?"
    B. "At which bank do you have a savings account?"
    C. "Do you have a savings account?"
    D. "May I assume that you have a savings account?"

6._____

7. You are interviewing a patient who is not cooperating to the extent necessary to get all required information. Therefore, you decide to be more forceful in your approach.
In this situation, such a course of action is

    A. *advisable,* because such a change in approach may help to increase the patient's participation
    B. *advisable,* because you will be using your authority more effectively
    C. *inadvisable,* because you will not be able to change this approach if it doesn't produce results
    D. *inadvisable,* because an aggressive approach generally reduces the validity of the interview

7._____

8. You have attempted to interview a patient on two separate occasions, and both attempts were unsuccessful. The patient has been totally uncooperative and you sense a personal hostility toward you.
Of the following, the BEST way to handle this type of situation would be to

    A. speak to the patient in a courteous manner and ask him to explain exactly what he dislikes about you
    B. inform the patient that you will not allow personality conflicts to disrupt the interview
    C. make no further attempt to interview the patient and recommend that he be billed in full
    D. discuss the problem with your supervisor and suggest that another investigator be assigned to try to interview the patient

8._____

9. At the beginning of an interview, a patient with normal vision tells you that he is reluctant to discuss his finances. You realize that it will be necessary in this case to ask detailed questions about his net income. When you begin this line of questioning, of the following, the LEAST important aspect you should consider is your

    A. precise wording of the question
    B. manner of questioning
    C. tone of voice
    D. facial expressions

9._____

10. A caseworker under your supervision has been assigned the task of interviewing a man who is applying for foster home placement for his two children. The caseworker seeks your advice as to how to question this man, stating that she finds the applicant to be a timid and self-conscious person who seems torn between the necessity of having to answer the worker's questions truthfully and the effect he thinks his answers will have on his application. Of the following, the BEST method for the caseworker to use in order to determine the essential facts in this case is to

10._____

A. assure the applicant that he need not worry since the majority of applications for foster home placement are approved

B. delay the applicant's narration of the facts important to the case until his embarrassment and fears have been overcome

C. ignore the statements made by the applicant and obtain all the required information from his friends and relatives

D. inform the applicant that all statements made by him will be verified and are subject to the law governing perjury

11. Assume that a worker is interviewing a boy in his assigned group in order to help him find a job. At the BEGINNING of the interview, the worker should

    11.____

A. suggest a possible job for the youth

B. refer the youth to an employment agency

C. discuss the youth's work history and skills with him

D. refer the youth to the manpower and career development agency

12. As part of the investigation to locate an absent father, you make a field visit to interview one of the father's friends. Before beginning the interview, you identify yourself to the friend and show him your official identification.
For you to do this is, generally,

    12.____

A. *good practice,* because the friend will have proof that you are authorized to make such confidential investigations

B. *poor practice,* because the friend may not answer your questions when he knows why you are interviewing him

C. *good practice,* because your supervisor can confirm from the friend that you actually made the interview

D. *poor practice,* because the friend may warn the absent father that your agency is looking for him

13. You are interviewing a client in his home as part of your investigation of an anonymous complaint that he has been receiving Medicaid fraudulently. During the interview, the client frequently interrupts your questions to discuss the hardships of his life and the bitterness he feels about his medical condition.
Of the following, the BEST way for you to deal with these discussions is to

    13.____

A. cut them off abruptly, since the client is probably just trying to avoid answering your questions

B. listen patiently, since these discussions may be helpful to the client and may give you information for your investigation

C. remind the client that you are investigating a complaint against him and he must answer directly

D. seek to gain the client's confidence by discussing any personal or medical problems which you yourself may have

14. While interviewing an absent father to determine his ability to pay child support, you realize that his answers to some of your questions contradict his answers to other questions.
Of the following, the BEST way for you to try to get accurate information from the father is to

    14.____

A. confront him with his contradictory answers and demand an explanation from him

B.  use your best judgment as to which of his answers are accurate and question him accordingly
C.  tell him that he has misunderstood your questions and that he must clarify his answers
D.  ask him the same questions in different words and follow up his answers with related questions

15. Assume that an applicant, obviously under a great deal of stress, talks continuously and rambles, making it difficult for you to determine the exact problem and her need. In order to make the interview more successful, it would be BEST for you to

15.____

A.  interrupt the applicant and ask her specific questions in order to get the information you need
B.  tell the applicant that her rambling may be a basic cause of her problem
C.  let the applicant continue talking as long as she wishes
D.  ask the applicant to get to the point because other people are waiting for you

16. A worker must be able to interview clients all day and still be able to listen and maintain interest.
Of the following, it is MOST important for you to show interest in the client because, if you appear interested,

16.____

A.  the client is more likely to appreciate your professional status
B.  the client is more likely to disclose a greater amount of information
C.  the client is less likely to tell lies
D.  you are more likely to gain your supervisor's approval

17. When you are interviewing clients, it is important to notice and record how they say what they say—angrily, nervously, or with "body English"—because these signs may

17.____

A.  tell you that the client's words are the opposite of what the client feels and you may need to dig to find out what those feelings are
B.  be the prelude to violent behavior which no aide is prepared to handle
C.  show that the client does not really deserve serious consideration
D.  be important later should you be asked to defend what you did for the client

18. The patient you are interviewing is reticent and guarded in responding to your questions. He is not providing the information needed to complete his application for medical assistance.
In this situation, the one of the following which is the most appropriate course of action for you to take FIRST is to

18.____

A.  end the interview and ask him to contact you when he is ready to answer your questions
B.  advise the patient that you cannot end the interview until he has provided all the information you need to complete the application
C.  emphasize to the patient the importance of the questions and the need to answer them in order to complete the application
D.  advise the patient that if he answers your questions the interview will be easier for both of you

19. At the end of an interview with a patient, he describes a problem he is having with his       19.____
teenage son, who is often truant and may be using narcotics. The patient asks you for
advice in handling his son.
Of the following, the MOST appropriate action for you to take is to

    A. make an appointment to see the patient and his son together
    B. give the patient a list of drug counseling programs to which he may refer his son
    C. suggest to the patient that his immediate concern should be his own hospitalization
       rather than his son's problem
    D. tell the patient that you are not qualified to assist him but will attempt to find out
       who can

20. A MOST appropriate condition in the use of direct questions to obtain personal data in an      20.____
interview is that, whenever possible,

    A. the direct questions be used only as a means of encouraging the person inter-
       viewed to talk about himself
    B. provision be made for recording the information
    C. the direct questions be used only after all other methods have failed
    D. the person being interviewed understands the reason for requesting the informa-
       tion

_____

# KEY (CORRECT ANSWERS)

| | | | | |
|---|---|---|---|---|
| 1. | D | | 11. | C |
| 2. | A | | 12. | A |
| 3. | A | | 13. | B |
| 4. | D | | 14. | D |
| 5. | A | | 15. | A |
| 6. | B | | 16. | B |
| 7. | A | | 17. | A |
| 8. | D | | 18. | C |
| 9. | A | | 19. | D |
| 10. | B | | 20. | D |

# PREPARING WRITTEN MATERIAL

# PARAGRAPH REARRANGEMENT
## COMMENTARY

The sentences which follow are in scrambled order. You are to rearrange them in proper order and indicate the letter choice containing the correct answer at the space at the right.

Each group of sentences in this section is actually a paragraph presented in scrambled order. Each sentence in the group has a place in that paragraph; no sentence is to be left out. You are to read each group of sentences and decide upon the best order in which to put the sentences so as to form as well-organized paragraph.

The questions in this section measure the ability to solve a problem when all the facts relevant to its solution are not given.

More specifically, certain positions of responsibility and authority require the employee to discover connections between events sometimes, apparently, unrelated. In order to do this, the employee will find it necessary to correctly infer that unspecified events have probably occurred or are likely to occur. This ability becomes especially important when action must be taken on incomplete information.

Accordingly, these questions require competitors to choose among several suggested alternatives, each of which presents a different sequential arrangement of the events. Competitors must choose the MOST logical of the suggested sequences.

In order to do so, they may be required to draw on general knowledge to infer missing concepts or events that are essential to sequencing the given events. Competitors should be careful to infer only what is essential to the sequence. The plausibility of the wrong alternatives will always require the inclusion of unlikely events or of additional chains of events which are NOT essential to sequencing the given events.

It's very important to remember that you are looking for the best of the four possible choices, and that the best choice of all may not even be one of the answers you're given to choose from.

There is no one right way to these problems. Many people have found it helpful to first write out the order of the sentences, as they would have arranged them, on their scrap paper before looking at the possible answers. If their optimum answer is there, this can save them some time. If it isn't, this method can still give insight into solving the problem. Others find it most helpful to just go through each of the possible choices, contrasting each as they go along. You should use whatever method feels comfortable, and works, for you.

While most of these types of questions are not that difficult, we've added a higher percentage of the difficult type, just to give you more practice. Usually there are only one or two questions on this section that contain such subtle distinctions that you're unable to answer confidently, and you then may find yourself stuck deciding between two possible choices, neither of which you're sure about.

----

# EXAMINATION SECTION
## TEST 1

DIRECTIONS: The sentences that follow are in scrambled order. You are to rearrange them in proper order and indicate the letter choice containing the correct answer. *PRINT THE LETTER OF THE CORRECT ANSWER IN THE SPACE AT THE RIGHT.*

1. Below are four statements labeled W., X., Y., and Z.           1.____
    W.   He was a strict and fanatic drillmaster.
    X.   The word is always used in a derogatory sense and generally shows resentment and anger on the part of the user.
    Y.   It is from the name of this Frenchman that we derive our English word, martinet.
    Z.   Jean Martinet was the Inspector-General of Infantry during the reign of King Louis XIV.

    The *PROPER* order in which these sentences should be placed in a paragraph is:

    A.  X, Z, W, Y        B.  X, Z, Y, W        C.  Z, W, Y, X        D.  Z, Y, W, X

2. In the following paragraph, the sentences which are numbered, have been jumbled.    2.____
    1.   Since then it has undergone changes.
    2.   It was incorporated in 1955 under the laws of the State of New York.
    3.   Its primary purpose, a cleaner city, has, however, remained the same.
    4.   The Citizens Committee works in cooperation with the Mayor's Inter-departmental Committee for a Clean City.

    The order in which these sentences should be arranged to form a well-organized paragraph is:

    A.  2, 4, 1, 3        B.  3, 4, 1, 2        C.  4, 2, 1, 3        D.  4, 3, 2, 1

Questions 3-5.

DIRECTIONS: The sentences listed below are part of a meaningful paragraph but they are not given in their proper order. You are to decide what would be the *best order* in which to put the sentences so as to form a well-organized paragraph. Each sentence has a place in the paragraph; there are no extra sentences. You are then to answer questions 3 to 5 inclusive on the basis of your rearrangements of these secrambled sentences into a properly organized paragraph.

In 1887 some insurance companies organized an Inspection Department to advise their clients on all phases of fire prevention and protection. Probably this has been due to the smaller annual fire losses in Great Britain than in the United States. It tests various fire prevention devices and appliances and determines manufacturing hazards and their safeguards. Fire research began earlier in the United States and is more advanced than in Great Britain. Later they established a laboratory specializing in electrical, mechanical, hydraulic, and chemical fields.

3. When the five sentences are arranged in proper order, the paragraph starts with the sentence which begins     3.\_\_\_\_

     A.   "In 1887 ..."      B.   "Probably this ..."      C.   "It tests ..."
     D.   "Fire research ..."      E.   "Later they ..."

4. In the last sentence listed above, "they" refers to     4.\_\_\_\_

     A.   insurance companies
     B.   the United States and Great Britain
     C.   the Inspection Department
     D.   clients
     E.   technicians

5. When the above paragraph is properly arranged, it ends with the words     5.\_\_\_\_

     A.   "... and protection."      B.   "... the United States."
     C.   "... their safeguards."      D.   "... in Great Britain."
     E.   "... chemical fields."

———

# KEY (CORRECT ANSWERS)

     1.   C
     2.   C
     3.   D
     4.   A
     5.   C

———

# TEST 2

DIRECTIONS: In each of the questions numbered 1 through 5, several sentences are given. For each question, choose as your answer the group of numbers that represents the *most logical* order of these sentences if they were arranged in paragraph form. *PRINT THE LETTER OF THE CORRECT ANSWER IN THE SPACE AT THE RIGHT.*

1. 1. It is established when one shows that the landlord has prevented the tenant's enjoyment of his interest in the property leased.
   2. Constructive eviction is the result of a breach of the covenant of quiet enjoyment implied in all leases.
   3. In some parts of the United States, it is not complete until the tenant vacates within a reasonable time.
   4. Generally, the acts must be of such serious and permanent character as to deny the tenant the enjoyment of his possessing rights.
   5. In this event, upon abandonment of the premises, the tenant's liability for that ceases.
   The CORRECT answer is:

   A. 2, 1, 4, 3, 5          B. 5, 2, 3, 1, 4          C. 4, 3, 1, 2, 5
   D. 1, 3, 5, 4, 2

   1.____

2. 1. The powerlessness before private and public authorities that is the typical experience of the slum tenant is reminiscent of the situation of blue-collar workers all through the nineteenth century.
   2. Similarly, in recent years, this chapter of history has been reopened by anti-poverty groups which have attempted to organize slum tenants to enable them to bargain collectively with their landlords about the conditions of their tenancies.
   3. It is familiar history that many of the workers remedied their condition by joining together and presenting their demands collectively.
   4. Like the workers, tenants are forced by the conditions of modern life into substantial dependence on these who possess great political arid economic power.
   5. What's more, the very fact of dependence coupled with an absence of education and self-confidence makes them hesitant and unable to stand up for what they need from those in power.
   The CORRECT answer is:

   A. 5, 4, 1, 2, 3          B. 2, 3, 1, 5, 4          C. 3, 1, 5, 4, 2
   D. 1, 4, 5, 3, 2

   2.____

3. 1. A railroad, for example, when not acting as a common carrier may contract; away responsibility for its own negligence.
   2. As to a landlord, however, no decision has been found relating to the legal effect of a clause shifting the statutory duty of repair to the tenant.
   3. The courts have not passed on the validity of clauses relieving the landlord of this duty and liability.
   4. They have, however, upheld the validity of exculpatory clauses in other types of contracts.
   5. Housing regulations impose a duty upon the landlord to maintain leased premises in safe condition.

   3.____

6.  As another example, a bailee may limit his liability except for gross negligence, willful acts, or fraud.
The CORRECT answer is:

A. 2, 1, 6, 4, 3, 5     B. 1, 3, 4, 5, 6, 2     C. 3, 5, 1, 4, 2, 6
D. 5, 3, 4, 1, 6, 2

4.  1.  Since there are only samples in the building, retail or consumer sales are generally eschewed by mart occupants, and,in some instances, rigid controls are maintained to limit entrance to the mart only to those persons engaged in retailing.     4.____
    2.  Since World War I, in many larger cities, there has developed a new type of property, called the mart building.
    3.  It can, therefore, be used by wholesalers and jobbers for the display of sample merchandise.
    4.  This type of building is most frequently a multi-storied, finished interior property which is a cross between a retail arcade and a loft building.
    5.  This limitation enables the mart occupants to ship the orders from another location after the retailer or dealer makes his selection from the samples.
The CORRECT answer is:

A. 2, 4, 3, 1, 5     B. 4, 3, 5, 1, 2     C. 1, 3, 2, 4, 5
D. 1, 4, 2, 3, 5

5.  1.  In general, staff-line friction reduces the distinctive contribution of staff personnel.     5.____
    2.  The conflicts, however, introduce an uncontrolled element into the managerial system.
    3.  On the other hand, the natural resistance of the line to staff innovations probably usefully restrains over-eager efforts to apply untested procedures on a large scale.
    4.  Under such conditions, it is difficult to know when valuable ideas are being sacrificed.
    5.  The relatively weak position of staff, requiring accommodation to the line, tends to restrict their ability to engage .in free, experimental innovation.
The CORRECT answer is:

A. 4, 2, 3, 1, 3     B. 1, 5, 3, 2, 4     C. 5, 3, 1, 2, 4
D. 2, 1, 4, 5, 3

―――――

# KEY (CORRECT ANSWERS)

1.  A
2.  D
3.  D
4.  A
5.  B

―――――

# TEST 3

DIRECTIONS:   Questions 1 through 4 consist of six sentences which can be arranged in a logical sequence. For each question, select the choice which places the numbered sentences in the *most logical* sequence. *PRINT THE LETTER OF THE CORRECT ANSWER IN THE SPACE AT THE RIGHT.*

1.   1.   The burden of proof as to each issue is determined before trial and remains upon the same party throughout the trial.      1.____
     2.   The jury is at liberty to believe one witness' testimony as against a number of contradictory witnesses.
     3.   In a civil case, the party bearing the burden of proof is required to prove his contention by a fair preponderance of the evidence.
     4.   However, it must be noted that a fair preponderance of evidence does not necessarily mean a greater number of witnesses.
     5.   The burden of proof is the burden which rests upon one of the parties to an action to persuade the trier of the facts, generally the jury, that a proposition he asserts is true.
     6.   If the evidence is equally balanced, or if it leaves the jury in such doubt as to be unable to decide the controversy either way, judgment must be given against the party upon whom the burden of proof rests.

The CORRECT answer is:

A.   3, 2, 5, 4, 1, 6        B.   1, 2, 6, 5, 3, 4        C.   3, 4, 5, 1, 2, 6
D.   5, 1, 3, 6, 4, 2

2.   1.   If a parent is without assets and is unemployed, he cannot be convicted of the crime of non-support of a child.      2.____
     2.   The term "sufficient ability" has been held to mean sufficient financial ability.
     3.   It does not matter if his unemployment is by choice or unavoidable circumstances.
     4.   If he fails to take any steps at all, he may be liable to prosecution for endangering the welfare of a child.
     5.   Under the penal law, a parent is responsible for the support of his minor child only if the parent is "of sufficient ability."
     6.   An indigent parent may meet his obligation by borrowing money or by seeking aid under the provisions of the Social Welfare Law.

The CORRECT answer is:

A.   6, 1, 5, 3, 2, 4        B.   1, 3, 5, 2, 4, 6        C.   5, 2, 1, 3, 6, 4
D.   1, 6, 4, 5, 2, 3

3.
1. Consider, for example, the case of a rabble rouser who urges a group of twenty people to go out and break the windows of a nearby factory.
2. Therefore, the law fills the indicated gap with the crime of inciting to riot."
3. A person is considered guilty of inciting to riot when he urges ten or more persons to engage in tumultuous and violent conduct of a kind likely to create public alarm.
4. However, if he has not obtained the cooperation of at least four people, he cannot be charged with unlawful assembly.
5. The charge of inciting to riot was added to the law to cover types of conduct which cannot be classified as either the crime of "riot" or the crime of "unlawful assembly."
6. If he acquires the acquiescence of at least four of them, he is guilty of unlawful assembly even if the project does not materialize.

The CORRECT answer is:

   A. 3, 5, 1, 6, 4, 2      B. 5, 1, 4, 6, 2, 3      C. 3, 4, 1, 5, 2, 6
   D. 5, 1, 4, 6, 3, 2

3.___

4.
1. If, however, the rebuttal evidence presents an issue of credibility, it is for the jury to determine whether the presumption has, in fact, been destroyed.
2. Once sufficient evidence to the contrary is introduced, the presumption disappears from the trial.
3. The effect of a presumption is to place the burden upon the adversary to come forward with evidence to rebut the presumption.
4. When a presumption is overcome and ceases to exist in the case, the fact or facts which gave rise to the presumption still remain.
5. Whether a presumption has been overcome is ordinarily a question for the court.
6. Such information may furnish a basis for a logical inference.

The CORRECT answer is:

   A. 4, 6, 2, 5, 1, 3      B. 3, 2, 5, 1, 4, 6      C. 5, 3, 6, 4, 2, 1
   D. 5, 4, 1, 2, 6, 3

4.___

———

# KEY (CORRECT ANSWERS)

1. D
2. C
3. A
4. B

———

# PREPARING WRITTEN MATERIAL

# EXAMINATION SECTION
## TEST 1

DIRECTIONS:   Each of Questions 1 through 5 consists of a sentence which may or may not
be an example of good formal English usage.

Examine each sentence, considering grammar, punctuation, spelling, capitalization, and
awkwardness. Then choose the correct statement about it from the four options below it.

If the English usage in the sentence given is better than any of the changes suggested in
options B, C, or D, pick option A. (Do not pick an option that will change the meaning of the
sentence.

1.   I don't know who could possibly of broken it.                                                 1.____

   A.   This is an example of good formal English usage.
   B.   The word "who" should be replaced by the word "whom."
   C.   The word "of" should be replaced by the word "have."
   D.   The word "broken" should be replaced by the word "broke."

2.   Telephoning is easier than to write.                                                          2.____

   A.   This is an example of good formal English usage.
   B.   The word "telephoning" should be spelled "telephoneing."
   C.   The word "than" should be replaced by the word "then."
   D.   The words "to write" should be replaced by the word "writing."

3.   The two operators who have been assigned to these consoles are on vacation.                    3.____

   A.   This is an example of good formal English usage.
   B.   A comma should be placed after the word "operators."
   C.   The word "who" should be replaced by the word "whom."
   D.   The word "are" should be replaced by the word "is."

4.   You were suppose to teach me how to operate a plugboard.                                       4.____

   A.   This is an example of good formal English usage.
   B.   The word "were" should be replaced by the word "was."
   C.   The word "suppose" should be replaced by the word "supposed."
   D.   The word "teach" should be replaced by the word "learn."

5.   If you had taken my advice; you would have spoken with him.                                    5.____

   A.   This is an example of good formal English usage.
   B.   The word "advice" should be spelled "advise."
   C.   The words "had taken" should be replaced by the word "take."
   D.   The semicolon should be changed to a comma.

# KEY (CORRECT ANSWERS)

1.  C
2.  D
3.  A
4.  C
5.  D

———

# TEST 2

DIRECTIONS:   Select the correct answer.

1.  The *one* of the following sentences which is *MOST* acceptable from the viewpoint of correct grammatical usage is:                                         1.____

    A.  I do not know which action will have worser results.
    B.  tie should of known better.
    C.  Both the officer on the scene, and his immediate supervisor, is charged with the responsibility.
    D.  An officer must have initiative because his supervisor will not always be available to answer questions.

2.  The *one* of the following sentences which is *MOST* acceptable from the viewpoint of correct grammatical usage is:                                         2.____

    A.  Of all the officers available, the better one for the job will be picked.
    B.  Strict orders were given to all the officers, except he.
    C.  Study of the law will enable you to perform your duties more efficiently.
    D.  It seems to me that you was wrong in failing to search the two men.

3.  The *one* of the following sentences which does *NOT* contain a misspelled word is:                                         3.____

    A.  The duties you will perform are similiar to the duties of a patrolman.
    B.  Officers must be constantly alert to sieze the initiative.
    C.  Officers in this organization are not entitled to special privileges.
    D.  Any changes in procedure will be announced publically.

4.  The *one* of the following sentences which does *NOT* contain a misspelled word is:                                         4.____

    A.  It will be to your advantage to keep your firearm in good working condition.
    B.  There are approximately fourty men on sick leave.
    C.  Your first duty will be to pursuade the person to obey the law.
    D.  Fires often begin in flameable material kept in lockers.

5.  The *one* of the following sentences which does *NOT* contain a misspelled word is:                                         5.____

    A.  Officers are not required to perform technical maintainance.
    B.  He violated the regulations on two occasions.
    C.  Every employee will be held responable for errors.
    D.  This was his nineth absence in a year.

————————

# KEY (CORRECT ANSWERS)

1. D
2. C
3. C
4. A
5. B

---

# TEST 3

DIRECTIONS:    Select the correct answer.

1.  You are answering a letter that was written on the letterhead of the ABC Company jind      1.____
    signed by James H. Wood, Treasurer. What is usually considered to be the correct salu-
    tation to use in your reply?

    A.  Dear ABC Company:        B.  Dear Sirs:
    C.  Dear Mr. Wood:           D.  Dear Mr. Treasurer:

2.  Assume that one of your duties is to handle routine letters of inquiry from the public.      2.____
    The one of the following which is usually considered to be *MOST* desirable in replying
    to such a letter is a

    A.  detailed answer handwritten on the original letter of inquiry
    B.  phone call, since you can cover details more easily over the phone than in a letter
    C.  short letter giving the specific information requested
    D.  long letter discussing all possible aspects of the question raised

3.  The *CHIEF* reason for dividing a letter into paragraphs is to      3.____

    A.  make the message clear to the reader by starting a new paragraph for each new
        topic
    B.  make a short letter occupy as much of the page as possible
    C.  keep the reader's attention by providing a pause from time to time
    D.  make the letter look neat and businesslike

4.  Your superior has asked you to send an e-mail from your agency to a government      4.____
    agency in another city. He has written out the message and has indicated the name of
    the government agency.
    When you dictate the message to your secretary, which of the following items that
    your superior has *NOT* mentioned must you be sure to *include*?

    A.  Today's date
    B.  The full address of the government agency
    C.  A polite opening such as "Dear Sirs"
    D.  A final sentence such as "We would appreciate hearing from your agency in reply
        as soon as is convenient for you"

5.  The one of the following sentence which is grammatically preferable to the others is:      5.____

    A.  Our engineers will go over your blueprints so that you may have no problems in
        construction.
    B.  For a long time he had been arguing that we, not he, are to blame for the confu-
        sion.
    C.  I worked on this automobile for two hours and still cannot find out what is wrong
        with it.
    D.  Accustomed to all kinds of hardships, fatigue seldom bothers veteran policemen.

# KEY (CORRECT ANSWERS)

1. C
2. C
3. A
4. B
5. A

———

# TEST 4

DIRECTIONS: Select the correct answer.

1. Suppose that an applicant for a job as snow laborer presents a letter from a former employer stating: "John Smith has a pleasing manner and never got into an argument with his fellow employees. He was never late or absent." This letter

   1._____

   A.  indicates that with some training Smith will make a good snow gang boss
   B.  presents no definite evidence of Smith's ability to do snow work
   C.  proves definitely that Smith has never done any snow work before
   D.  proves definitely that Smith will do better than average work as a snow laborer

2. Suppose you must write a letter to a local organization in your section refusing a request in connection with collection of their refuse.
You should *start* the letter by

   2._____

   A.  explaining in detail the consideration you gave the request
   B.  praising the organization for its service to the community
   C.  quoting the regulation which forbids granting the request
   D.  stating your regret that the request cannot be granted

3. Suppose a citizen writes in for information as to whether or not he may sweep refuse into the gutter. A Sanitation officer answers as follows:
Dear Sir:

   3._____

     No person is permitted to litter, sweep, throw or cast, or direct, suffer or permit any person under his control to litter, sweep, throw or cast any ashes, garbage, paper, dust, or other rubbish or refuse into any public street or place, vacant lot, air shaft, areaway, backyard or court.

                                       Very truly yours,
                                       John Doe

This letter is *poorly* written *CHIEFLY* because

   A.  the opening is not indented
   B.  the thought is not clear
   C.  the tone is too formal and cold
   D.  there are too many commas used

4. A section of a disciplinary report written by a Sanitation officer states: "It is requested that subject Sanitation man be advised that his future activities be directed towards reducing his recurrent tardiness else disciplinary action will be initiated which may result in summary discharge." This section of the report is *poorly* written *MAINLY* because

   4._____

   A.  at least one word is misspelled
   B.  it is not simply expressed
   C.  more than one idea is expressed
   D.  the purpose is not stated

5.  A section of a disciplinary report written by an officer states: "He comes in late. He takes      5.\_\_\_\_
    too much time for lunch. He is lazy. I recommend his services be dispensed with."
    This section of the report is *poorly* written *MAINLY* because

    A.  it ends with a preposition
    B.  it is not well organized
    C.  no supporting facts are stated
    D.  the sentences are too simple

---

# KEY (CORRECT ANSWERS)

1.  B
2.  D
3.  C
4.  B
5.  C

---

# ANSWER SHEET

TEST NO. _____ PART _____ TITLE OF POSITION _____

PLACE OF EXAMINATION _____ DATE _____

(CITY OR TOWN)                                    (STATE)

RATING

---

## USE THE SPECIAL PENCIL.   MAKE GLOSSY BLACK MARKS.

| | A B C D E | | A B C D E | | A B C D E | | A B C D E | | A B C D E |
|---|---|---|---|---|---|---|---|---|---|---|
| 1 | ⁞⁞ ⁞⁞ ⁞⁞ ⁞⁞ ⁞⁞ | 26 | ⁞⁞ ⁞⁞ ⁞⁞ ⁞⁞ ⁞⁞ | 51 | ⁞⁞ ⁞⁞ ⁞⁞ ⁞⁞ ⁞⁞ | 76 | ⁞⁞ ⁞⁞ ⁞⁞ ⁞⁞ ⁞⁞ | 101 | ⁞⁞ ⁞⁞ ⁞⁞ ⁞⁞ ⁞⁞ |
| 2 | | 27 | | 52 | | 77 | | 102 | |
| 3 | | 28 | | 53 | | 78 | | 103 | |
| 4 | | 29 | | 54 | | 79 | | 104 | |
| 5 | | 30 | | 55 | | 80 | | 105 | |
| 6 | | 31 | | 56 | | 81 | | 106 | |
| 7 | | 32 | | 57 | | 82 | | 107 | |
| 8 | | 33 | | 58 | | 83 | | 108 | |
| 9 | | 34 | | 59 | | 84 | | 109 | |
| 10 | | 35 | | 60 | | 85 | | 110 | |

Make only ONE mark for each answer.   Additional and stray marks may be
counted as mistakes.   In making corrections, erase errors COMPLETELY.

| | A B C D E | | A B C D E | | A B C D E | | A B C D E | | A B C D E |
|---|---|---|---|---|---|---|---|---|---|---|
| 11 | ⁞⁞ ⁞⁞ ⁞⁞ ⁞⁞ ⁞⁞ | 36 | ⁞⁞ ⁞⁞ ⁞⁞ ⁞⁞ ⁞⁞ | 61 | ⁞⁞ ⁞⁞ ⁞⁞ ⁞⁞ ⁞⁞ | 86 | ⁞⁞ ⁞⁞ ⁞⁞ ⁞⁞ ⁞⁞ | 111 | ⁞⁞ ⁞⁞ ⁞⁞ ⁞⁞ ⁞⁞ |
| 12 | | 37 | | 62 | | 87 | | 112 | |
| 13 | | 38 | | 63 | | 88 | | 113 | |
| 14 | | 39 | | 64 | | 89 | | 114 | |
| 15 | | 40 | | 65 | | 90 | | 115 | |
| 16 | | 41 | | 66 | | 91 | | 116 | |
| 17 | | 42 | | 67 | | 92 | | 117 | |
| 18 | | 43 | | 68 | | 93 | | 118 | |
| 19 | | 44 | | 69 | | 94 | | 119 | |
| 20 | | 45 | | 70 | | 95 | | 120 | |
| 21 | | 46 | | 71 | | 96 | | 121 | |
| 22 | | 47 | | 72 | | 97 | | 122 | |
| 23 | | 48 | | 73 | | 98 | | 123 | |
| 24 | | 49 | | 74 | | 99 | | 124 | |
| 25 | | 50 | | 75 | | 100 | | 125 | |

# ANSWER SHEET

TEST NO. _____ PART _____ TITLE OF POSITION _____

PLACE OF EXAMINATION _____ DATE _____

(CITY OR TOWN)          (STATE)

| RATING |
| --- |
| |

## USE THE SPECIAL PENCIL.  MAKE GLOSSY BLACK MARKS.

(Answer grid, questions 1–125, each with options A B C D E)

1  2  3  4  5  6  7  8  9  10

**Make only ONE mark for each answer.  Additional and stray marks may be counted as mistakes.  In making corrections, erase errors COMPLETELY.**

11 12 13 14 15 16 17 18 19 20 21 22 23 24 25

26 27 28 29 30 31 32 33 34 35 36 37 38 39 40 41 42 43 44 45 46 47 48 49 50

51 52 53 54 55 56 57 58 59 60 61 62 63 64 65 66 67 68 69 70 71 72 73 74 75

76 77 78 79 80 81 82 83 84 85 86 87 88 89 90 91 92 93 94 95 96 97 98 99 100

101 102 103 104 105 106 107 108 109 110 111 112 113 114 115 116 117 118 119 120 121 122 123 124 125